Today, when Christians are broadsided by suffering, they are often counseled to avoid negative thoughts, buffer themselves with time off, exercise, and seek out supportive relationships. Sadly, the God of the Bible and *His* counsel is often left out of the "treatment plan." That's why I *love* Mike Fabarez's new book *Lifelines for Tough Times*. He writes not only from decades of hard study, but from the heartache of personal experience—thus, his words carry *weight*. If you are looking for the right perspective when things go wrong—very wrong—then *Lifelines* is a must-read. I highly recommend this powerful and insightful book!

Joni Eareckson Tada
Founder, Joni and Friends International Disability Center

Why is there so much pain and suffering in the world? Why do God's people suffer so much, even while it seems the wicked prosper? How can we trust God through times of torment and pain—especially when it seems as if He is impervious to our prayers? And why does He sometimes delay answering?

The Bible gives answers to those questions and many others like them. Better yet, God Himself has made rock-solid promises that give us ground to stand on even when our questions can't be answered. Mike Fabarez carefully, thoroughly expounds the biblical principles and promises that offer help in those times of oppressive darkness. If you are seeking ways to encourage friends in turmoil, and especially if you are in the throes of some trial in your own life, you will find this book a wonderful and welcome resource.

John MacArthur
Pastor-Teacher, Grace Community Church, Sun Valley, CA
President, Master's College and Seminary

Pastor Mike speaks with such clarity and helpful insights on the subject of suffering and pain. Why am I suffering? Does God really care? Is He really in control? How should I live in the midst of my pain? The biblical wisdom and concrete examples in *Lifelines for Tough Times* will bring encouragement and hope to those who are having to navigate their own season of suffering.

Josh McDowell
Christian Apologist; Founder, Josh McDowell Ministry

Pastor Mike Fabarez's new book is rich in biblical insights on the problem of pain and suffering in the Christian life. Writing with the sensitivity of a pastor, Fabarez shows us how to attain an empowering spiritual perspective to help us rise above life's tough times. I heartily recommend his book and pray that it finds a wide audience.

Ron Rhodes
Author, President of Reasoning from the Scriptures Ministries

Mike Fabarez writes with a perfect balance of heart, soul, and mind. He understands the hurts and hopes of the human experience, while providing real biblical solutions to our deepest needs and most profound struggles. Don't miss this powerful, helpful, and insightful book. God will use it to stir your soul and change your life.

Dr. Ed Hindson
Assistant Chancellor, Liberty University, Lynchburg, VA

It has been said that life is ten percent what you make it, and ninety percent how you take it. If that is true then how one handles suffering will determine to a great extent the quality of one's life and legacy. *Lifelines for Tough Times* by my friend Mike Fabarez is a book that will help you do just that. Written by someone who knows his Bible and the subject of suffering firsthand, this book teaches you how not to waste your sorrows. The blessing of this book is that it is God-centered in its focus, biblical in its content, real in its approach, and eminently practical in its use. Buy it, read it, and learn how to remain whole in a broken world.

Philip De Courcy
Senior Pastor, Kindred Community Church, Anaheim, CA
Teacher on daily radio broadcast *Know the Truth*

People have struggles. This book has answers. Not easy, pat answers, but answers that have been forged from years of time in God's Word and its application to trials Mike and his family have faced. *Lifelines for Tough Times* comes from the heart of a pastor and strikes a beautiful balance between biblical content and pastoral comfort. In these pages you will find biblical truth for your head and thoughtful application for your heart. Nothing is more important in times of trial than keeping the faith. In this book you have the opportunity to sit at the feet of someone who's been there and done it by God's grace.

Mark Hitchcock
Senior Pastor, Faith Bible Church, Edmond, OK
Associate Professor of Bible Exposition, Dallas Theological Seminary

We all face seasons of great difficulty—with sometimes overwhelming and almost crushing trials. For some, these last longer than a season. What matters is how we respond to what we face. How can we experience God's presence, help, and encouragement as we walk through a long, dark valley? How can we be faithful to God? How can we simply hold on? Pastor Mike Fabarez gives us biblically rooted perspective on facing tough times. This is not merely theoretical. Mike has lived this and shares candidly from his own life experience. What he says will resonate with your soul and will help keep you centered in God's loving arms and purposes as you face life's issues.

Clinton E. Arnold
Dean and Professor of New Testament,
Talbot School of Theology (Biola University)

Mike's book is sorely needed today as people inside and outside of the church are struggling to make sense of the suffering that seemingly slams into our lives unannounced. Mike unravels some of the mystery by taking a bigger step back from our immediate pain and helping us to see what the real purpose in life is. And Mike is not writing from the safety and comfort of his theological ivory tower. He shares his own journey of pain and confusion through the birth of his severely handicapped daughter that forced him and his wife to wrestle through the questions of pain and God's sovereignty. The book lovingly and biblically lays the foundation for making sense out of suffering while avoiding superficial clichés that only rub salt in the wound. His explanation of what it means that the Spirit groans with us in prayer in Romans 8:26 is worth the price of the book. This book gives real comfort, as it connects us to a real God and His purposes.

Brad Bigney
Senior Pastor, Grace Fellowship Church, Florence, KY

Mike Fabarez is one of my favorite Bible teachers. When it comes to tough times, Mike writes as an expert and fellow traveler. If you've ever wondered, "Where is God, and what is He up to?" *Lifelines for Tough Times* is the book for you.

Hal Seed
Author; Founding Pastor, New Song Community Church,
Oceanside, CA

There is only one thing that can be said about a book dealing with this subject—it is timely.

All of us have tough times and need to be able to handle them God's way. So…the message is always timely. But there is a greater problem for our country—and Christians in particular—at present: the growing opposition to the faith, and the likelihood of persecution spreading throughout our land. Who knows how this will pan out? But it is not too soon for believers to begin thinking about the possibilities and how they will face them.

In both personal difficulties and in those which might come to the church in general, we must be prepared. This book is designed to help—and it will.

Jay Adams
Author; Founder, Christian Counseling and Educational Foundation

LIFELINES
for
TOUGH TIMES

MIKE FABAREZ

HARVEST HOUSE PUBLISHERS
EUGENE, OREGON

LIFELINES FOR TOUGH TIMES

Copyright © 2014 by Mike Fabarez
Published by Harvest House Publishers
Eugene, Oregon 97402
www.harvesthousepublishers.com

Library of Congress Cataloging-in-Publication Data
    Fabarez, Michael, 1964-
    Lifelines for tough times / Mike Fabarez.
      pages cm
    ISBN 978-0-7369-5816-5 (pbk.)
    ISBN 978-0-7369-5817-2 (eBook)
    1. Suffering—Religious aspects—Christianity. I. Title.
    BV4909.F33 2014
    248.8'6—dc23

2013045581

CONTENTS

Finding Genuine Help in Life's Pain

It's one thing to give thought to the puzzling question of pain and suffering in light of the existence of a good and loving God, as though we were high school students struggling to make sense of our algebra homework. It is an entirely different kind of struggle when our lives suddenly (or perhaps gradually) take a left turn and we have to navigate our way in the midst of excruciating pain or prolonged suffering.

While I have admittedly written this book for those who are searching for hope in the middle of a dark and difficult period of their lives, I should be up front and tell you that we will have to grapple with a little *algebra* along the way. You see, a long series of cheerful platitudes won't provide any lasting help when we find ourselves tearfully asking why God would allow us to face difficult trials and how is it that he expects us to get through them all. Real strength and perspective will come only when we are willing to calibrate our thoughts and align our lives with the truth that God has revealed in his Word.

God has much to say about why things are not the way they ought to be, and how it is that we, as his beloved children, can "walk through the valley of the shadow of death" and actually "fear no evil"

(Psalm 23:4). And we will take a fresh look at several of the Bible's timeless truths—truths that have provided profound comfort and genuine help for generations of God's people through the centuries.

As a pastor of a large church for many years, I have walked through crushing hurts and heartbreaking losses with a variety of people—some whose trust in God has been refined and who come out of their trials stronger and wiser, as well as others who have spiraled downward into increasing anger and frustration and ended up walking away from Christ altogether.

Much is riding on how you and I handle life's pain. For Christians, there should be only one choice. Because, as Peter said when Jesus asked if he too was going to walk away, "Lord, to whom shall we go? You have the words of eternal life" (John 6:68). Jesus provided ample proof that he has the answers—for this life and the next. The resurrected Christ knows what we need when we are suffering. Walking away is not an option. Deepening our understanding, refining our faith, and learning how to respond realistically is our agenda in the pages ahead.

Not only have I walked through a variety of trials with the people I love in my church, but I have also had to navigate some dark days in my own family. I will elaborate on one particular season that is arguably more painful than when the problem is embedded in our own bodies. The struggles my wife and I faced with the unexpected diagnosis regarding our only daughter was what God used to take many of his eternal principles off the inspired pages and into the center of our daily lives.

So join me as we look to God and his truth to give us strength, perspective, and hope as we consider the problem of pain and the genuine solutions found only in Christ.

CHAPTER 1

Things Will Go Wrong

For us it began with a routine ultrasound. We were expecting our third child. With two rambunctious little boys at home, Carlynn and I had selfishly prayed that this child would be a girl. But like so many other expectant parents, our prayers always ended with the admission that it really didn't matter—boy or girl, we just appealed to God for a healthy baby.

The ultrasound technician had been our longtime acquaintance, and knew we were hoping to hear the news that we could paint the nursery pink. As the goopy transducer scanned my wife's belly, all eyes were fixed on the grey haze on the computer screen. A smile spread across the tech's face as she exclaimed, "Yes, it's a girl!"

We were thrilled. We whispered our first prayer of joyful thanksgiving for our long-expected little girl, who, in anticipation years earlier, we had named Stephanie. But before we could say "Amen," the room grew strangely quiet. Our friend's smile disappeared. Her face was suddenly crestfallen. "I need to get the doctor," she said as she scurried out of the room.

The three-minute wait felt like hours.

What's wrong? How serious is it? Could we have somehow misunderstood what had just happened? Is our daughter okay?

The doctor walked in, quickly taking the controls of the ultrasound. He leaned into the display monitor. "We have a serious problem here," he said with a tone of sobriety we had never heard from him before. "Look here," he directed us. "This area of the cranium where you see black—it should be grey. The fetus is missing its brain. This is an anomaly called *anencephaly*. The fetus will certainly not survive. We need to schedule an abortion."

We were stunned. A mix of emotions flooded our hearts.

To us, Stephanie was so much more than a "fetus." This was the daughter we had prayed about for many years. Add to that, I had already been a senior pastor for more than ten years and took a firm public stance against abortion. So for us, the doctor's words were like fingers on a chalkboard. Abortion!

Carlynn and I looked at each other speechless. Without a word, we could each see the other draw on years of commitment to protecting human life. We were resolved. We would no more entertain the idea of abortion in this situation than if our four-year-old son were diagnosed with a terminal disease. We would see this pregnancy through come what may.

But we knew that with such a resolve we were entering a tumultuous season of grief and uncertainty. Our lives had just taken a left turn. Without warning, everything had changed. We were about to begin a journey punctuated by a series of victories and a sequence of defeats. We were about to travel an unfamiliar road filled with a depth of pain we had never experienced.

And we knew our pain was not unique.

No Exemptions

As a pastor for more than twenty-five years, I have had a front-row seat to the kinds of suffering and pain that flood Christians' lives. Sincerely loving God and tirelessly serving him obviously provide no exemption from pain. At any given time in a church like ours, the daily e-mails we receive listing the trials, heartaches, and diseases among our people chronicles a directory of suffering that is difficult to read, let alone pray through.

It is common for Christians to assume that a person's pains and difficulties have been brought on by some secret sin in his or her life. Perhaps there is some personal act of rebellion that God is responding to. Maybe there is a character flaw that is being addressed.

Such misguided thinking is one reason God gave us the book of Job. Remember how Job is described at the beginning of his painful excursion? He "was blameless and upright, one who feared God and turned away from evil" (Job 1:1). And that wasn't an assessment from just anyone. This evaluation came from God himself (cf. Job 1:8). We know from the rest of Scripture that Job, like everyone else on the planet, was not perfect. But the onslaught of pain Job faced had nothing to do with God's frustration toward him. Job was a paragon of righteous living, yet he suffered greatly. All his children died in a catastrophic storm. All his businesses went bankrupt. He was struck with a debilitating disease, and his reputation was trashed. Job's wife was less than supportive of him, and his friends accused him of hidden, unconfessed sin.

Though God eventually restored Job's fortunes, the suffering he endured was very real. His memories included the funerals of his children. His body bore the scars of an amazingly difficult season of life. And this happened to one who was described by God as one of the godliest individuals in the Old Testament.

A Misguided Assumption

Why all the pain? If God loves his people, why doesn't he guard them from all the hurt? You might be able to figure out some specific answers for Job's excruciating season of pain. But even in his case, there are many head-scratching aspects to the story. Especially if your assumption is that if God loves his children he will keep them from suffering and pain. After all, isn't that the way we parent? Because we love our kids, if we had the power to prevent a disease, or the opportunity to exempt them from broken bones, we would certainly exercise that power. We would keep them from pain. We would exempt them from suffering. Makes sense, doesn't it? If you look around, you'll find this is the foundational assumption of most people in our world.

In her autobiography, President George W. Bush's wife Laura speaks of driving through a stop sign at age seventeen and colliding with the car of her classmate, Michael Douglas, which resulted in his death. Laura says she pleaded with God for her friend's life, to no avail. She writes,

> I lost my faith that November, lost it for many, many years. It was the first time that I had prayed to God for something, begged him for something, not the simple childhood wishing on a star but humbly begging for another human life. And it was as if no one heard. My begging, to my seventeen-year-old mind, had made no difference. The only answer was the sound of Mrs. Douglas's sobs on the other side of that thin emergency room curtain.[1]

Mrs. Bush eloquently verbalizes what so many others have confessed to me over the years. Namely, that their frustration and disappointment with God, because he had "failed" to protect them from life's tragedies, had driven them to "lose their faith."

In a way, this can be a good thing. Not that they are upset with God, but that their unbiblical assumptions about God are revealed and forced to change. For if our "faith" has been in a "god" who is presupposed to exempt us from life's pain and suffering, then it is a faith that needs to be lost. It needs to be exchanged for a biblical faith in the real God.

As we learn in the case of Job, the real God is a God who not only has the power to prevent our pain; he is also a God who is fully aware of our pain. And God, as we consistently see in the Bible, is a God who strategically and thoughtfully prescribes our pain.

Such prescriptions do not contradict his love for us or his dedication to our well-being. That may be hard to fathom. (My attempts to resolve this seeming contradiction is one of the reasons I have wanted to write this book.) But we need to see the reality that these truths do not contradict each other.

Even as God's children we will face difficult and painful experiences in our lives. Consequently, we cannot afford to function with a distorted and simplistic view of God, a view that assumes our pain means he is either powerless to stop it, ignorant that we are experiencing it, or in some way slack in fulfilling a presumed promise that he would never allow pain, suffering, or tragedy to touch us. The truth is, God not only allows pain, he has actually planned it and even promised it. Even so, we must remember that our God is a good God. He has a purpose in the pain and stakes his character on the truth that in the end he works all things together for good for those who love him and are called according to his purpose (Romans 8:28). That gives us hope, even when the pain is severe and the world seems out of control.

> Because sin became a part of the human equation, suffering is a part of the human experience.

A Broken World

We live in a sinful, fallen, and broken world. The origin of all this is described for us in Genesis 3. There we find some initial answers to why we suffer. As unsatisfying as it may be to read, this chapter of the Bible details the purposeful introduction of suffering, pain, disease, and death. Here in the middle of God's statements to the first man and woman, we see that God is the one who is personally imposing these painful realities:

> To the woman he said, "I will surely multiply your pain in childbearing; in pain you shall bring forth children..."

> And to Adam he said, "Because you have listened to the
> voice of your wife and have eaten of the tree of which I
> commanded you, 'You shall not eat of it,' cursed is the
> ground because of you; in pain you shall eat of it all the
> days of your life; thorns and thistles it shall bring forth
> for you...By the sweat of your face you shall eat bread,
> till you return to the ground, for out of it you were taken;
> for you are dust, and to dust you shall return" (Genesis
> 3:16-19).

Adam and Eve's fatal choice to eat from a prohibited tree careened the human race into a host of painful consequences, the most serious of which is death itself. As Romans 6:23 says, "The wages of sin is death."

Because sin became a part of the human equation, suffering is a part of the human experience. That may seem over the top, but the Bible couldn't be clearer. The original human decision to disregard God's command resulted in a promise from God that every person, regardless of his or her relative piety, would encounter pain, disease, and death. There are several paradoxical glimpses of grace in this reality that we will examine later, but for now let us concede that the pain and suffering we so naturally deplore was imposed on the human race by God in response to human sin.

Think of it this way: If we didn't experience suffering, pain, disease, and death, God would be unfaithful to his promise that there would be consequences if Adam and Eve disobeyed him. He would be dishonest. In the words of the theologian Don Carson, "this perennial slide toward death with all its associated illness, death and bereavement is nothing other than the outworking of God's judicial sentence, 'when you eat of it you will certainly die' (Genesis 2:17)."[2]

Therefore, our suffering—and even our death—are not signs that things are out of control and that God is absent or silent. No, the unpleasant realities of pain and loss are signs that everything is right on schedule. They are reminders that God is in control and accomplishing precisely what he has said is supposed to happen.

God's Promise to Fix the Problem

At this point some will object and suggest that I have overlooked a large portion of the Bible—the positive, hopeful portion. Doesn't the Bible tell us that God is the problem solver? Doesn't it say that he heals, delivers us, and fixes our circumstances?

Yes it does. But we need to be clear about timing. The sweeping and all-encompassing promises about God making "every crooked thing straight"[3] and "wiping away every tear"[4] are directed to a time when "the kingdom of the world has become the kingdom of our Lord and of his Christ" (Revelation 11:15). The root of the problem of sin, suffering, and death were dealt with at the first coming of Jesus Christ, but their eradication must wait for his second coming. Jesus paid the price to redeem his people and forgive their sins, but he has yet to reverse all of the effects of sin and the consequences he has imposed on this fallen world.

Even for those who have repented of their sins and placed their trust in Christ to forgive their sins, the judicial response of God on the human race has not yet been revoked. And until the second coming of Christ, we are all still members of fallen humanity. The godly and ungodly will all physically suffer, become sick, and eventually die.

There are times when God does graciously deliver, mercifully heal, and kindly stave off the peril of death, but it is always a temporary reprieve. The final reversal of death, the permanent elimination of disease, and the complete abolition of suffering must wait for the next world. We must always be careful to not claim promises before their time. Jesus often sought to get this point fixed in our minds. For instance, he said, "In the world you will have tribulation. But take heart; I have overcome the world" (John 16:33). All the work that is required to reverse the problems we face has been accomplished, but God has reserved the implementation of his perfect blessings for a future time.

For those of us who are trusting in Christ, we can be sure God will fix our problems. We will reign with Christ (Revelation 22:3). We will have bodies which are impervious to disease (1 Corinthians 15:42-43). We will never attend another funeral (Isaiah 25:8). Mourning, crying, and pain will be things of the past (Revelation 21:4). There will be no more war, conflict, or battles (Isaiah 2:4). Life will be good. Perfect, in fact.

But for now, we must prepare ourselves for the path this side of the coming kingdom. As Paul encouraged the first-century Christians, we should "continue in the faith" knowing that "through many tribulations we must enter the kingdom of God" (Acts 14:22).

Hostility Against Christians

It doesn't help that there are many who peddle a brand of Christianity that is supposed to cure all our ills and fulfill all our earthly dreams. Their hypocrisy should be evident, for eventually every peddler of a health-and-wealth gospel ends up dying and leaving behind all their assets. But many flock to hear these charlatans in the hopes that adding Christ to their lives will fix all their temporal problems.

However, the truth is that adding Christ to your life creates a number of temporal problems. Think about it: Non-Christians may struggle with all the same problems as Christians; they may struggle with disease, disappointment, and death, but at least the culture is tailored to help them drown their sorrows, numb their pain, and muddy their fears regarding their own mortality. In other words, the world suits them. It's a place they can fit in and find outlets for their desires and priorities. We who are Christians, on the other hand, have the problem of not fitting in. The culture in which we are called to live out our Christianity rejects us in many ways. Not only is the culture not Christian, it is hostile to our priorities and values. Jesus put it this way:

> If the world hates you, know that it has hated me before it hated you. If you were of the world, the world would love you as its own; but because you are not of the world, but I chose you out of the world, therefore the world hates you. Remember the word that I said to you: "A servant is not greater than his master." If they persecuted me, they will also persecute you. If they kept my word, they will also keep yours (John 15:18-20).

Who as a Christian hasn't experienced the jeers, criticisms, and putdowns that come when we openly confess our trust and allegiance to Jesus Christ? To freely affirm that we read and study the Bible as God's revelation and our binding guidebook for life will raise eyebrows in some settings and invite outright insults in others. Budding friendships can come to a screeching halt, clients can suddenly decide to seek another vendor, and an assortment of disparaging comments can flow from people "who can't stand 'religious' people" or "will never do business again with a Christian." While in the modern West we may not be fed to literal lions, there is certainly a cultural price to pay if we are willing to stand up and speak out about our commitment to Christ.

Jesus told us to expect such hostility, and to even rejoice over it. He said,

> Blessed are you when others revile you and persecute you and utter all kinds of evil against you falsely on my account. Rejoice and be glad, for your reward is great in heaven, for so they persecuted the prophets who were before you (Matthew 5:11-12).

This kind of ridicule can be gladly endured, knowing that we are not only being lumped in together with the great men and women of the Bible and church history, but that we are also being aligned with Christ himself. It will still hurt, and it may have financial or relational repercussions, but at least we know it is something that every godly person is called to bear.

Spiritual Enemies

As Christians we not only face incompatibility with the world, but much like in the case of Job, we also have a spiritual enemy. God's ultimate and most powerful adversary, along with all his henchmen, make it their job to oppose us in every way possible. We are told that as Christians, God's formidable antagonist has become ours: "Your adversary the devil prowls around like a roaring lion, seeking someone to devour" (1 Peter 5:8).

The Bible calls our adversary the "destroyer" (the meaning of "Apollyon" in Revelation 9:11), a "slanderer" (the term translated "devil" meaning "slanderer" in Luke 4:2, 13), the "deceiver" (Revelation 12:9), the "tempter" (Matthew 4:3), and our "accuser" (Revelation 12:10). None of this is good. And it brings to mind the ways our lives are made more difficult as a result of our alliance with Christ.

Often we do not connect the dots in our thinking, but it is safe to assume that some of the destruction, slander, opposition, temptations, and accusations that we endure as Christians have more behind them than meets the eye. The Bible asserts that these spiritual enemies of ours are real, and that they are focused on causing real trouble, doubt, and discouragement in our lives.

But what about Christ's protection? Doesn't the Bible say that "he who is in you [i.e., God's Spirit] is greater than he who is in the world [i.e., Satan]"?[5] Yes it does, and yes he is. God is infinitely greater and more powerful than our spiritual enemies. But while we can be sure that Satan and his henchmen will not carry out all that they'd like to do in our lives, we must realize that—as evidenced throughout the Bible—God does not grant some kind of all-inclusive buffer of protection from their activity. Job is a classic example of Satan's destructive activity in the life of one of God's beloved followers. But he is not our only example.

Consider Paul's chronic illness, mentioned in 2 Corinthians 12. He doesn't reveal what the ailment is. All we know is that it's annoying and painful like a "thorn" and that it is sent by Satan (verse 7). The amazing thing about this confession is that Paul says he had repeatedly asked God to remove this ailment, and God said no. Paul went on to conclude that his "thorn from Satan" was a purposeful provision from God. In his case we learn that God's prescription of pain was an effective safeguard against pride.[6] So, while Jesus has promised to "never leave you nor forsake you,"[7] at the same time, you are not fully insulated from the enemy's harassment. "For indeed, all who desire to live a godly life in Christ Jesus will be persecuted" (2 Timothy 3:12).

> Every true Christian will experience the continual conflict between *who* they are (new creatures in Christ) and *what* they are (fallen human beings).

An Internal Struggle

There is yet another type of problem that God said we would all face—one that hits very close to home. It is one thing to encounter problems externally from the world, our anti-Christian culture, or even demonically instigated troubles. But we also need to be prepared to experience a set of struggles that come from within us. I'm talking about the conflict that occurs between a Christian's regenerated, reborn, redeemed spirit and the sinful flesh or fallen humanity in which our spirit is encased.

Every true Christian will experience the continual conflict between *who* they are (new creatures in Christ) and *what* they are (fallen human beings). Perhaps 1 Peter 2:11 summarizes it best when it tells us that we are to "abstain from the passions of the flesh, which wage war against your soul." Any time there is a "waging of war," you can change your caricatures of idyllic, easy, breezy Christianity to the biblical motifs of battle, warfare, and struggle.

That may not fit the Sunday school images of the Christian life
or the assumptions of Psalm 23 with the smiling Good Shepherd
and his frolicking sheep. But as long as that image is now in your
mind, let's consider this motif for a moment. If we are to think of
ourselves as God's sheep, let's be careful to add to that picture the
promise that we will be surrounded by "wolves" and that we will be
made to walk "through the valley of the shadow of death." Then we
must also remember that sheep are animals who have a tendency to
wander away. They have conflicting motivations. While sheep do
have a true loyalty to their shepherd and they hear his voice and follow him, in their sheepishness, they also desire to forge their own
path. They desire in their sheepish curiosity to do their own thing,
thereby transgressing the call and leadership of their shepherd.

Real Christians have heard Christ's voice and have, by God's
regenerative work, chosen to follow him. But they are still encased
in their humanness, which is stubborn, independent, and at odds
with their loyalty to follow Christ. Our human and fleshly desires
are at war within us. The Holy Spirit is present in our lives to direct,
discipline, and empower our obedience to our Good Shepherd, but
the flesh fights, claws, and opposes the Spirit's influence on our
spirit. A daily war is inevitable. As Paul wrote, "The desires of the
flesh are against the Spirit, and the desires of the Spirit are against the
flesh, for these are opposed to each other" (Galatians 5:17). Thankfully this conflict is one that God will aid us in fighting, but it's still
a fight—at times, a painfully big one.

Put it all together, and the biblical picture of the Christian life
looks a lot different than what we often hear or want to imagine.
A.W. Tozer was right to tell us:

> To bring ourselves under the plenary authority of Jesus
> Christ…is to invite trouble from a hostile world…Add
> to this the temptations of the devil and a lifelong strug-
> gle with the flesh and it will be obvious that we will need

to defer most of our enjoyments to a more appropriate time.[8]

Adjusting Expectations

All of this unpleasant focus on the downside of the present reality for Christians should settle one thing for good—we shouldn't expect a pain-free, problem-free Christian life. I can't emphasize this enough: Changing that expectation changes a lot!

When Jesus called his disciples by saying, "If anyone would come after me, let him deny himself and take up his cross and follow me,"[9] there should have been no confusion about what taking this path would entail. The "narrow way"[10] Jesus spoke of is not a primrose path. It does end with incomparable treasures as we "enter by the narrow gate,"[11] but the journey will necessarily include a variety of thorns, internal conflicts, jeers from the world, opposition from Satan, and a share of strategic trials handpicked for us by God. These are not signs that something is wrong; they are the bumps that remind us that we are on the right path.

Pressing On

It was admittedly difficult for my wife and I to see the terminal diagnosis of our preborn daughter as "an expected bump," but there was no other option. We knew that God was neither unaware of the problem, nor was he impotent to have prevented it. We loved God and we knew he loved us. We could only tearfully embrace the news as something that God had sovereignly chosen for us, and for Stephanie. After all, he had never promised there would be a tomorrow for us or our children. He never promised that my wife and I would have healthy babies. There were no guarantees from heaven that our earthly families would be free from pain, disease, or death. Having officiated funerals of young children from solid Christian families over the years, I knew that we carried no special exemptions.

As God would have it for Stephanie, pain and disease were her immediate realities, but death was off the table, at least for the time being. Our doctor's snap diagnosis was less than accurate. Stephanie's brain did in fact form, but it had been severely compressed due to the swollen ventricles in her brain. As a specialist pointed out to us, she did not have anencephaly; she had hydrocephalous—sometimes called "water on the brain." In her case this threatening problem was caused by a failure of some of her vertebrae to properly form, allowing an abnormal protrusion of the spinal cord from her spinal column. That, in turn, herniated the rear portion of her brain, sealing off the drainage path for her ventricles and inflating them to an abnormal size.

This congenital disorder of the vertebrae is called spina bifida, which comes in a variety of degrees of severity. Throughout a series of prenatal appointments the outlook for Stephanie was mixed. There were lots of guesses and prognoses, which seemed to always include words like *retardation, paralysis, malformation, wheelchairs, surgeries, therapies, catheters, leg braces* and occasionally we'd still hear the word *stillbirth*. We'd have to wait and see the full extent of what God's path would be for her and for our family. But come what may, we were committed to pressing on with faith in a good God. We were ready to walk this unfamiliar road that God had prescribed for us, knowing that he would walk it with us and that he was able to sustain us each step of the way.

Your Trial

You or someone you love might not currently be facing a medical crisis. Instead, perhaps your pain is the distress of financial trouble, the grief of personal loss, the hurt of relational conflict, or the ache of rejection. Whatever it may be, remember that the Lord has promised to be "near to the brokenhearted" (Psalm 34:18). His desire is to walk with you through your trial.

C.S. Lewis insightfully wrote that "God whispers to us in our pleasures…but shouts in our pain."[12] My prayer is that we are all careful to listen. We must not allow our pain to deafen us to the instruction of God and the lessons he desires to impart. We dare not put our head down and trudge through each painful day without looking up. God desires to be near to you in your trials, but he requires that you draw near to him (James 4:8).

> The path may be unpleasant, but the destination will not disappoint.

So don't let the pain harden your heart. Be attentive to God's wisdom and hopeful in your suffering. Know that he is a loving Father who "saves the crushed in spirit" (Psalm 34:17). He has a plan for you, and he is working it out. The path may be unpleasant, but the destination will not disappoint.

CHAPTER 2

The Pain You Can Change

Have you ever had a broken bone? Ouch—it's awful. I've experienced that several times. Growing up I fractured bones on the ball field, on the playground, and at home in an infamous tussle with my older brother. It's one thing to have your bones broken "by accident," but it's an entirely different matter to have them broken on purpose! And I'm not referring to the incident with my brother (he claims he didn't mean to do it).

After one particularly awkward spill on the playground, which resulted in a snapped radius and ulna, I remember the doctor giving me stern instructions about the importance of keeping my arm immobilized in its new cast. I didn't listen. I hated the restrictions. I continued to lift, push, and pull everything my childhood threshold of pain could endure.

When it came time for my checkup with the doctor, he X-rayed my forearm, examined the films, then called in my mother to announce to us that there was a problem, and that an adjustment was needed.

An adjustment? I thought. That sounded simple enough. Maybe a new coat of plaster, or an added layer of cotton where the cast kept scratching my palm. But of course, that's not what he meant. The doctor went on to explain that the bones in my forearm had fused together incorrectly because of my disregard of his instructions, and so they needed to be reset. *Reset.* That was code for "I have to break your arm, kid." After sawing the cast in two and firmly taking hold of the two separated halves still attached to my arm, he glanced at the X-ray, and—crack!—he broke my arm. On purpose! I'll never forget it.

And I will also never forget, as he began to repair the sawn cast that encased my newly rebroken arm, how he looked at me with a crinkled brow and said, "Now listen, son. Like I said before, don't use your arm for the next six weeks!"

Divinely Broken Bones

In Psalm 51 David talked about the pain of his broken bones—not the accidentally fractured components of his physical body, but the aspects of his personal life that had been intentionally broken by the God who loved him. You see, Psalm 51 is about the painful yet purposeful discipline that the Lord had imposed on David's life after his sexual affair with Bathsheba. In this song to God, David recognized that the troubles he had experienced in the wake of his sin were "the bones that *you* [God] have broken" (verse 8). Elsewhere regarding the same situation he spoke of God's "hand" pressed against him, sapping his energy, strength, and joy until he rightly recognized his transgression for what it was (Psalm 32:3-5).

Now here's a critically important biblical truth that is so often overlooked or dismissed by people because it is incompatible with their understanding of a loving God: *Sometimes the Lord, in his love, deliberately brings pain and suffering into our lives in order to lead us to confess and forsake our sin.*

God imposing pain in the lives of his own children? "Impossible!" some would protest. But as we will see, this is not only exactly what the Bible teaches, it is also one of the most demonstrative expressions of God's love for us. And what a glaring oversight it would be for me to have you search for help and hope amid your suffering without having you consider your current pain in light of this frequently highlighted biblical reality.

Of course, not all the difficulties, suffering, and pain in our lives are related to our wrongdoing. But sometimes when things become rigidly crooked due to our sinful choices, our heavenly Father, the Great Physician, steps in to make things straight. And that "resetting" hurts.

A Father's Discipline

In the book of Hebrews we learn that God is a disciplinarian. The modern parental mind-set may be indulgent and permissive, but our heavenly Father loves us enough to correct us. Back in a time when consistent parental discipline was more likely than it is today, the author of Hebrews wrote,

> We have had earthly fathers who disciplined us and we respected them. Shall we not much more be subject to the Father of spirits and live? For they disciplined us for a short time as it seemed best to them, but he disciplines us for our good, that we may share his holiness. For the moment all discipline seems painful rather than pleasant, but later it yields the peaceful fruit of righteousness to those who have been trained by it (12:9-11).

Your childhood may not have benefited from this endangered blessing. Or perhaps instead of receiving thoughtful and measured discipline, you grew up with a kind of angry parental retaliation that failed to engender any "respect" for your mom and dad. In either case, you may not be able to fully appreciate the powerful analogy presented in this passage.

Godly discipline springs primarily from sorrow and grief rather than annoyance and spite.

Thankfully, I know the value of being raised by loving disciplinarians. And if you do too, you can join me in affirming that unpleasant consequences and loving concern are not mutually exclusive.

A caring father is able to envision the irreparable damage that can come from unchecked disobedience. That is why he will work diligently to bring correction to a defiant child. When a verbal reprimand fails to modify his child's behavior, he realizes that increasingly painful consequences are necessary. Not because he is angry, capricious, or vindictive, but because he loves his child enough to correct him or her.

So it is with God, Hebrews 12 tells us. Holiness in our lives is the desired goal (verse 10), and if a "reproof" doesn't bring us to repentance (verse 5), then some sort of "painful" discipline may be carried out (verse 11). As with any loving parent, this kind of godly discipline springs primarily from sorrow and grief rather than annoyance and spite. The Bible tells us that our transgressions "grieve the Holy Spirit of God, by whom [we] were sealed for the day of redemption" (Ephesians 4:30).

As paradoxical as it may seem, the withholding of discipline is not an indication of God's kindness toward us. The book of Proverbs goes so far as to say to earthly parents that refraining from discipline is a sign that they "hate" their children (13:24). The book of Hebrews points out that the only reason we would go without some periodic expressions of God's painful discipline is because we are not really Christians after all.

> The Lord disciplines the one he loves, and chastises every
> son whom he receives. It is for discipline that you have
> to endure. God is treating you as sons. For what son is
> there whom his father does not discipline? If you are left
> without discipline, in which all have participated, then
> you are illegitimate children and not sons (12:6-8).

Your current trial may have nothing to do with God's correction.

But if by the end of this chapter you realize that it may in fact be an expression of the Lord's discipline, take heart, for it is a pain you can change.

The Many Forms of God's Discipline

The dreaded instrument of correction hung on a nail in the closet of our back porch. It was blue, made of a thick semitransparent plastic. It was about the size and shape of a ping-pong paddle, but when mom or dad walked back to retrieve it, we knew it was no game. When "the paddle" came out, the Fabarez boys knew it was time for some serious soul-searching.

However, for God's children, the form of discipline God might use is not as predictable. The Bible shows us that the Lord's discipline comes in a variety of forms. The only common feature, according to Hebrews 12:11, is that "all discipline seems painful rather than pleasant." So when life takes a left turn and pleasant times are replaced by painful experiences, we would be wise to honestly consider our lives to see if there is some pattern of sin we've been ignoring, or some call to obedience we've been disregarding. Let's look at a few biblical examples of the forms God's discipline can take.

1. Financial Problems

Five hundred years before the coming of Christ the Israelites were commissioned by God to rebuild the temple. It had been destroyed 70 years earlier by the Babylonians. The command was simple enough. But like many of God's instructions, obedience required a thoughtful, prioritized, sacrificial effort to get the job done. And with so many other things clamoring for Israel's attention—like setting up and customizing their own houses in the newly resettled land—the call to reconstruct their worship center was increasingly neglected.

God then sent his prophet to call the people to repent. "Is it time for you yourselves to dwell in your paneled houses," Haggai asked, "while [God's] house lies in ruins?" (Haggai 1:4) This is a sermon that shouldn't have been needed, because, according to the rest of Haggai's message, God had been disciplining his people through a painful season of financial problems.

> Consider your ways. You have sown much, and harvested little…he who earns wages does so to put them into a bag with holes…You looked for much, and behold, it came to little. And when you brought it home, I blew it away. Why? declares the LORD of hosts. Because of my house that lies in ruins, while each of you busies himself with his own house (Haggai 1:5-6, 9).

Imagine yourself a part of this group. You've hit some financially difficult times. You've worked hard at your job, but you and your family never seem to have enough money at the end of each month. You keep putting your money in your checking account, but it drains out like water through a colander. You just aren't able to make ends meet. So what do you do?

A lot of Christians just plow on ahead. They work harder. They redouble their efforts. They cut back on their monthly expenditures. They go to a Christian budgeting seminar. They read a book on financial planning. They pray for God's blessing and keep on trying to get ahead. But if their financial difficulties are a result God's discipline, none of their remedies will ever work. Not until they realize "God's hand pressing against them"—specifically against their finances—will the situation change.

Likewise, the Israelites continued to face discipline because they failed to make the connection between their financial troubles and their disobedience to God's clear instructions.

2. Health Problems

In the first-century church of Corinth, Christians had turned the practice of the Lord's Supper into a frivolous, self-serving potluck. A scheduled church party with a lot of free food had replaced any spirit of sober and grateful reflection on the substitutionary death of Christ on the cross. The record of Christ's instructions regarding this memorial meal was crystal clear, and the Corinthians had surely heard it taught many times. But their desire to have "a good time of fellowship" overshadowed the biblical commands.

The Christians in Corinth were disobedient and Paul wrote to call them to repentance. However, this part of his letter shouldn't have been necessary. The people should have recognized their transgression, for God had been actively disciplining them—not with financial troubles, but with health problems. The apostle Paul rebuked the Corinthian believers for their flippant approach to the communion service, and he pointed out the connection between their epidemic health problems and their disobedience:

> Anyone who eats and drinks without discerning the body eats and drinks judgment on himself. That is why many of you are weak and ill, and some have died. But if we judged ourselves truly, we would not be judged. But when we are judged by the Lord, we are disciplined so that we may not be condemned along with the world (1 Corinthians 11:29-32).

Imagine a health crisis sweeping through your church. What are the common Christian responses? Doctor's visits, more vitamins, a growing list for the weekly prayer meeting, and a lot of chicken soup being passed around. But in this case, because the health problems were a means of God's discipline, none of that was going to reverse the downward spiral. The "hand of God" was against the health of God's people in Corinth. And that was only going to be remedied by soul-searching, repentance, and a turning away from their selfish perversion of the Lord's Supper.

3. Emotional Pain

In Psalm 51:8, David poetically equated God's discipline in his life to divinely "broken bones." In Psalm 32:3-4 he spoke of his "bones wasted away," "groaning," and "strength...dried up." This should give us some indication of the internal pain God may bring our way to get us to confess and forsake our sin. I think we can all attest that David's descriptive phrases accurately capture the pain and guilt we've felt in the wake of our sinful decisions.

When we are not quick to confess and forsake our sin, God's Spirit is faithful to compound these natural feelings of guilt with his added conviction that is impossible to ignore. It flavors all that we do. It drains our spirit and, as David suggested, it is as though God turns up the temperature, and we are made to live day after day in the stifling heat of a summer afternoon (Psalm 32:4). This kind of emotional pain makes everyday activities seem like drudgery.

Haggai said it is like eating a meal and never being satisfied, or putting on a comfy coat but never getting comfortable (Haggai 1:6). This general dissatisfaction is something we have all experienced. And God's Word would lead us to conclude that sometimes this emotional pain is sent by God as his loving discipline to get us to see some particular sin in our lives for what it is.

Again, consider what often happens when Christians encounter this internal pain and discomfort. How often do we rush to find physical, psychological, or pharmaceutical remedies, when in fact what is really needed is a time of soul-searching that makes us say with David, "Search me, O God, and know my heart! Try me and know my thoughts! And see if there be any grievous way in me, and lead me in the way everlasting!" (Psalm 139:23-24).

We could look at many more examples of "painful rather than pleasant" experiences that God has and does use as forms of discipline. But I trust these few biblical examples are sufficient to heighten your awareness of what God might do in our lives. God loves us so much, and he so intensely desires that we reflect more and more of his holiness in our lives, that when we neglect his truth and disregard his biblical instructions, he will bring painful circumstances into our lives in an effort to get us to see the problem and make the correction.

Of course, not every financial problem, illness, emotional pain, or unpleasant experience is an expression of God's discipline. And the majority of this book is about the unpleasant circumstances that are *not* a result of his discipline. But before we see how to keep faith in the midst of those, we need to rule out that our current "tough time" isn't a form of God's loving discipline.

Search Me, Oh God

As a parent, when I find it necessary to discipline one of my erring children, there is one thing I desperately want to communicate—the reason! I don't want there to be any mystery about the reason for the pain that I have sanctioned. My goal in discipline is for them to see their disobedience for what it is, own it, and be "impressed" enough by the discomfort to not repeat the offense.

It's no different in our relationship with God. When we suffer pain because of a wayward action, we can be sure God wants us to know exactly what our defiant action is. There is a simple yet surprisingly difficult way to find out.

In Psalm 139 there is a question that gets us to the heart of the matter in no time. David taught us to pray:

> Search me, O God, and know my heart! Try me and know my thoughts! And see if there be any grievous way in me, and lead me in the way everlasting! (verses 23-24).

These words are easy to repeat, but they require some uncommon honesty to be useful. In our day, when society has all but abandoned any sense of personal responsibility, and when everyone seems to have an excuse or justification for their wrong behavior, it is hard for Christians to practice true honesty and admit fault for anything. The biblical record contains its fair share of excuse-makers as well. Adam was quick to blame Eve, and Eve was quick to blame the tempter (Genesis 3:11-13). And sometimes even when the right question is asked, the biblical characters aren't quick to contemplate the potential answers.

Consider the army of Israel some eleven centuries before Christ. The Philistines "drew up in line against Israel, and when the battle spread, Israel was defeated" (1 Samuel 4:2). God's people were unable to defend themselves and were beaten by their enemies. And the losses were big. About 4000 Jewish soldiers were killed.

The suffering that day apparently prompted the people to ask the right question. They asked, "Why has the LORD defeated us today before the Philistines?" (verse 3). That was a good place to start. The problem was they apparently never truly contemplated the potential answers; they were quick to propose a remedy that showed they didn't even consider there might be a reason the Lord had permitted their loss. They said, "Let us bring the ark of the covenant of the LORD here from Shiloh, that it may come among us and save us from the power of our enemy."

The consequences of doing this were disastrous. The Israelites marched right back into battle hoping for God's support, and were defeated a second time. Worse yet, the ark of the covenant was captured. Had the Israelites taken the time to ask God to search their hearts and their consciences, surely God would have directed them to the real problem—a compromising and rebellious priesthood that needed to be replaced.

So if you find yourself in a season of pain, loss, suffering, or defeat, spend time in prayer. Honestly and sincerely ask your heavenly Father to bring his specific conviction to your conscience. Ask him if in fact your unpleasant circumstances are the result of his discipline. Don't rush through this time of prayer too quickly. Ask that the Holy Spirit would help you discover any area of rebellion, disobedience, or indifference to his commands.

What to Look For

Obviously we should be responsive to any sinful activity that comes to mind when we ask God to search our hearts. But if you are thinking, *God is so holy, surely half the things I do fall short of his righteous standards,* don't lose heart. Think more specifically. God's discipline is not arbitrary. It usually comes as a result of a particular sinful problem.

When the writer of Hebrews offers his helpful instruction on the Lord's correction in Hebrews 12, he draws our attention to a few categories of sin that often trigger God's discipline.

1. Habitual Sins

Hebrews 12:1 speaks of the "sin which clings so closely." That is, sin that entangles us. Of course this may be a different sin for each Christian, but one thing is the same—it keeps on happening. It's a recurring transgression that never seems far from us. It "clings so closely" to us no matter how many times we regret it. Certainly God wants us to have victory over such sins. And if our repeated cycle of temptation, failure, conviction, and confession doesn't eventually stop, we can count on God to step in to raise this problem to the top of our priority list.

So when you ask God to let you know whether your suffering is his discipline, be extraordinarily sensitive to any recurring patterns of sin in your life. Such habitual sin may be the reason God is intervening. He may want to show you that your current strategy for dealing with this sin is not working, and that a new strategy is required. He may even be prompting you to call out for some help from your brothers or sisters in Christ.

2. Giving Up

We are told in Hebrews 12 that Christ is the ultimate example of a righteous person who was willing to endure intense opposition in order to do what he was called to do. He didn't give up just because obedience became costly. The writer of Hebrews tells you to remember the example of Christ's perseverance "so that you may not grow weary or fainthearted" (verse 3).

Think about the various commands that the Bible clearly calls us to obey. We have heard the sermons, read the passages, felt the conviction, and set out to do them. We could be thinking of prayer, Bible study, worship, fellowship, evangelism, or giving. We know what God wants us to do, and most of us have a history of doing them. But sometimes doing the right thing becomes difficult or costly, and we grow weary and give up.

When that happens, we need to remember James 4:17: "Whoever knows the right thing to do and fails to do it, for him it is sin." If we are truly God's kids, our disregard for the things we once did obediently but have now abandoned will become a cause for God's discipline.

When you ask God to show you if there is "any grievous way"[1] in you, be quick to recognize any pangs of conviction that relate to giving up on what you know is right. As Jesus said, "Remember therefore from where you have fallen; repent, and do the works you did at first" (Revelation 2:5).

3. Unwilling to Struggle

Christians often use the word *struggle*, but not in the way it is used in Hebrews 12. When we say, "I'm struggling with sin," we usually mean "I've been sinning a lot." But the writer of Hebrews defines *struggle* as the pain involved in choosing *not* to sin. He prompts his readers to think about how much they are willing to suffer as they resolve to say "No!" to temptation. Unfortunately, for a lot of us, it's not much. Or maybe I should say it's not enough.

> God's will for us is to do the right thing no matter what it may cost us—even if it is life itself.

"Well, how far should we go?" you may ask. The writer of Hebrews provides us with a dramatic answer: "In your struggle against sin you have not yet resisted to the point of shedding blood" (Hebrews 12:4). Wow! Martyrdom is his challenge.

Resisting temptation is painful. It is a struggle. We can all recall a situation that brought intense discomfort when we resisted wrong and chose what was right. But there are few, if any Christians, who have avoided sin to the point of spilling their blood. Hebrews 12 tells us that we ought to be willing to go to such extremes. God's will for us is to do the right thing no matter what it may cost us—even if it is life itself. Frequently we possess that kind of resolve early in our Christian life, but as time goes on, our resolve wanes. And before we know it, we have to admit that our resistance to temptation can be breached with the slightest of pains.

When asking God to search you and try you to determine if you are being disciplined, be sensitive to any growing unwillingness to struggle to do what is right. Honestly consider if your threshold for giving in to sin has dropped to a new low in your life.

It's possible you may not need much direction once you honestly open yourself up to the Spirit's conviction. But if at first you draw a blank, remember to honestly reflect on the presence of any habitual sins, any areas of obedience you've recently given up on, and any overall change in your resolve to do right no matter what it takes. If at this point you can clearly identify the problem, be encouraged, for the remedy changes everything.

Confession and Repentance

The goal of God's discipline is our increasing holiness and something he calls "the peaceful fruit of righteousness" (Hebrews 12:11). When we admit the presence of sin in our lives and turn from it the sin ends, the discipline is lifted, and relational peace is restored. While the discipline brought on by our sin doesn't end our relationship with God, our transgressions certainly create a tension, which is immediately resolved when we sincerely see our sin for what it is and choose to forsake it.

God repeatedly reminds us that "whoever conceals his transgression will not prosper, but he who confesses and forsakes them will obtain mercy" (Proverbs 28:13). The Lord is eager to restore harmonious fellowship with his children who admit their iniquity. "If we confess our sins, he is faithful and just to forgive our sins and to cleanse us from all unrighteousness" (1 John 1:9). The word that is translated "confess" in the New Testament means "to agree with" God, or literally "to say the same thing" that he says about the problem. When we identify our sin, we need to sincerely agree with God that we have sinned—no excuses or rationalization. Just agree with him that it is wrong, and determine that you will renounce it.

We may tend to think of repentance as the biblical appeal to non-Christians, and so it is. But the call to repent is also directed at Christians who have fallen into sin. Christ uses the word eight times in the second and third chapters of Revelation as he explains the discipline he has brought to his churches, and will continue to bring, if they don't turn from their sins. That's what repentance is all about—turning from our sins!

Agreeing with God about sin and turning from it will make all the difference. This is God's objective when he imposes his loving discipline. We can be confident that our confession and repentance is the prescription that will bring an end to God's discipline. We are then left to embrace God's forgiveness and to celebrate his generous grace and mercy. With David we can sing, "Let me hear joy and gladness; let the bones that you have broken rejoice" (Psalm 51:8).

Lingering Consequences

It would be easy for me to recount the times during my childhood when my relationship with my parents was genuinely and completely restored after their discipline had prompted my sincere repentance. On some of those occasions, that was the end of the story. But at other times, it wasn't. The windows I broke with balls, bats, and golf clubs might be a good example. Of course I had been told not to hit balls toward the house, and throwing bats and golf clubs was prohibited. And so when I disobeyed and broke their windows, I was disciplined. That usually led to a genuine change of heart, along with my parents' generous forgiveness.

But my parents understandably made me pony up the money to get the windows fixed. The last time I remember, I was even made to learn how to cut the glass and do the installation myself. What it cost me in terms of money, time, and effort wasn't discipline, penance, or punishment. Those costs were simply my parents' way of providing me with reasonable consequences for the damage I had caused.

While we can safely assume that our confession and repentance brings God's discipline to an end, I must add the footnote that there may be lingering consequences that result from the damage we have caused. For instance, when David finally came clean about his sin with Bathsheba, he experienced a profound transformation in his relationship with God:

> When I kept silent, my bones wasted away through my groaning all day long. For day and night your hand was heavy upon me; my strength was dried up as by the heat of summer. I acknowledged my sin to you, and I did not cover my iniquity; I said, "I will confess my transgressions to the LORD," and you forgave the iniquity of my sin (Psalm 32:3-5).

But that was not the end of the story. There were many costly consequences associated with the damage David had caused. The sowing and reaping related to his scheming and sexual deviance lasted for many years, and adversely affected many members of his family. But much like learning to cut glass and putty a window with my father's help on a hot summer afternoon, the lingering consequences associated with our sin can be faced shoulder-to-shoulder with our heavenly Father's help.

It May Not Be Discipline

When we as Christians suffer, it is good for us to learn to ask, "Is this pain caused by my sin?" Even so, we can be sure the answer is not always yes. That's a good starting point when it comes to assessing why we are suffering. But as we observed earlier, not all suffering is caused by God's discipline. In fact, much of it isn't.

For example, when Jesus and the disciples encountered a blind man, the disciples looked to Jesus and asked, "Rabbi, who sinned, this man or his parents, that he was born blind?" (John 9:2). While there are examples of God striking people with blindness for their sin (e.g., Genesis 19:11; Deuteronomy 28:28), and while in a few years Jesus would impose a temporary blindness on the future apostle Paul for his persecution of the church (Acts 9:4-9), in this case Jesus said, "It was not that this man sinned, or his parents, but that the works of God might be displayed in him" (John 9:3).

Much of the suffering we face as Christians has nothing to do with sin—whether our own or the sin of our family. As we learned in the first chapter, a lot of the pain, loss, and disappointment we experience is because we live in a fallen world, encounter the hostility and treachery of evil people, and face a diversity of spiritual battles—not to mention the variety of ways that the Lord brings trials and testing into our lives to cause growth and build character.

As was the case with my daughter's life-threatening diagnosis, your season of suffering, pain, or loss may not be related to God's correction. Like us, once you rule out divine discipline, you may be left asking, "Why?" and wondering what God's purpose could possibly be. And that can be a good thing. Because asking those kinds of questions with an open Bible and a receptive heart can lead to a profound shift in your thinking. It can even change how you understand the whole point of Christianity.

CHAPTER 3

Shifting Your Focus Amid the Hurt

When the news of our daughter's prenatal diagnosis of spina bifida and hydrocephalus circulated through the church, many Christians added their voices to ours and prayed for little Stephanie. We heard it often: "I am praying for her, and for your whole family!" But exactly what was everyone asking God to do? Many, as you might expect, simply asked God to "fix the problem." "Heal her, Lord!" they would pray. Among them were a number of Christians with great faith, who fervently interceded in hopes that Stephanie's diagnosis would be reversed.

But that was not the only kind of prayer we heard. Nor was that the only sort of prayer Carlynn and I learned to pray during those difficult days.

A Human Inclination

Wanting the all-powerful God to fix our problems is certainly the most natural response to a painful crisis. We'd all prefer to live pain- and trouble-free. Unfortunately, it's easy for us to let this preference become our supreme goal. In the words of Thomas Jefferson, most people appear to believe that "the art of life is the art of avoiding pain."[1] That may be our natural inclination, but it certainly isn't how the Bible advises us to live. If success is to be measured by the avoidance of pain, then we are all failures—you, me, Jefferson, and most importantly, Jesus Christ himself.

The truth is that God's plans for us include episodes, seasons, and sometimes even a lifetime of pain. Hundreds of years before the arrival of Christ it was prophesied that he would be "a man of sorrows, and acquainted with grief" (Isaiah 53:3). His earthly mission, after all, included a supremely important appointment with the torturous pain of a Roman execution rack—"even death on a cross" (Philippians 2:8). And when Jesus gathered the crowds around himself, he was careful to disclose that God's path for every Christian would include the taking up of a cross of their own (Mark 8:34).

Understanding that God's plan for our lives will involve painful circumstances certainly shouldn't stop us from asking God to fix our problems and alleviate our pain. This too is a proper human inclination, which we see expressed in godly people throughout the Bible. We even witness it in Christ's prayers. As Jesus anticipated the excruciating pain of the cross while praying in the Garden of Gethsemane, he expressed these heartfelt words:

> He said to [Peter, James and John], "My soul is very sorrowful, even to death. Remain here and watch." And going a little farther, he fell on the ground and prayed that, if it were possible, the hour might pass from him. And he said, "Abba, Father, all things are possible for you. Remove this cup from me" (Mark 14:34-36).

And when struck with a painful, chronic ailment, the apostle Paul "pleaded with the Lord" repeatedly "that it should leave" him (2 Corinthians 12:8). But like Jesus, Paul soon concluded that his painful circumstance was strategically prescribed by God. So Paul echoed the sentiment of Christ's final line from that Gethsemane prayer: "Yet not what I will, but what you will" (Mark 14:36). So if your natural inclination to cry out for relief has resulted in "unanswered prayers," then you are in good company. And it's time to shift your focus as well as your prayers.

A Different Objective and Another Kind of Prayer

Following a slew of tests, and after all the medical specialists had weighed in, it became clear that our daughter's situation was, medically speaking, irreversible. The threatening effects we witnessed on the ultrasound were the consequence of physical defects that had formed during Stephanie's prenatal development months prior to their discovery. Of course God possesses the ability to raise the dead and create things out of nothing—and he has done so in some very special cases in biblical history. But like so many other parents dealing with congenital defects, we soon recognized that surgeries needed to be scheduled, and that some serious physical challenges would be a part of the cross our daughter and our family would have to bear. And accepting the reality of the problem we faced led us to change the way we prayed.

It is interesting to note that we have record of only a single instance in which Christ prayed in hopes of avoiding the unthinkable pain of the cross. And when Paul tells us of his "pleading with the Lord" for relief from his ailment, he said he only did so "three times" (2 Corinthians 12:8). I find we often take a lot longer than the godly examples in the Bible to shift our prayers from "fix my problem, Lord" to the kind of prayers we are about to discuss.

> Once we recognize that our goal as Christians cannot be to avoid pain, we must look to what God said about the goals he has called us to.

Obviously there are things for which we should never stop praying. In some situations we need to persist and endure in protracted and prolonged praying (for example, Luke 18:1-7). But when it comes to pain and suffering, the Bible often chides us for not recognizing their necessary and strategic role in our Christian lives (1 Peter 4:12; James 1:2).

Shifting our focus and prayers begins with affirming some of the main reasons for why we exist in the first place. Once we recognize that our goal as Christians cannot be to avoid pain, we must look to what God said about the goals he has called us to. These are the ultimate priorities that won't be mutually exclusive to suffering. Actually, in many cases our suffering will not only help us achieve these goals; in fact, the suffering will often give us opportunities to achieve them in a way that we never could have without the crisis. Knowing these goals is essential.

Called to Glorify God

There are times in a baseball game when a pitcher will deliberately and strategically walk a batter. Usually it's because he wants to avoid dangerous hitters who can get runs on the scoreboard, and instead, go after a weaker hitter who is next up. Sometimes, for good reason, a coach will order a batter to bunt, even if that means the batter will likely be thrown out at first. The coach's goal is to advance runners who are already on base in the hopes of generating more runs. In both instances an "up-front sacrifice" is made by the pitcher and batter in the hopes of a better outcome for the whole team. This concept of keeping a bigger goal in mind at the expense of one's own statistics applies to the Christian life as well.

The Bible is clear—we exist to glorify God. That is why people were created. That is why you and I exist. And this should be our ultimate goal in all that we do. But what does that really mean? And how can we glorify God when we are hurting?

Unfortunately, if there was ever a word that seems lost in the jargon of Christian vocabulary, it would have to be the word *glory*. We hear it a lot in church and we read it often in the Bible, but it is hard to truly aim at glorifying God if we don't really know what it means.

In the original text of the Old Testament, the Hebrew word that is usually translated "glory" could more literally be translated "weighty" or "heavy." That may sound odd, but it is helpful. Think about the old '70s phrase "That's heavy, man!" We picture a long-haired guy in a tie-dyed shirt describing something that's important, serious, or significant. We still use forms of that word picture when we talk about a "weighty" topic or the "gravity" of a situation.

The Bible says there may be a lot of "glorious" things in heaven and on earth, but none of them can be compared to the importance, seriousness, and significance of God himself. We are told that "his glory is above the earth and heaven" (Psalm 148:13 NKJV), meaning that he is the greatest and most important being in the universe. We are also called to "give glory to the LORD God" (Joshua 7:19)—that is, we should cast the spotlight on him with our words and worship, telling ourselves and others that he is the greatest and most important being in the universe. And perhaps most challenging, we are called to "do all to the glory of God" with our actions (1 Corinthians 10:31), meaning that what we do and how we live ought to show that we understand that God is the most exalted being in the universe.

In goods times or bad, you and I exist to understand something of God's surpassing glory. We are to engage in giving God glory through our worshipful prayers and songs, and to live in such a way that we glorify God by showing that we know what and who is really most important. Sometimes the Coach is determined to accomplish that goal through us while we walk a batter or get thrown out at first base. His agenda is bigger than our personal statistics.

When we fail to be mindful of God's incomparable glory, we quickly begin to assume that our lives are about our own importance, our own significance, our own pleasure, and our own happiness. Then when we encounter painful situations that God does not immediately remove even after we've asked him to, we find ourselves lacking motivation for glorifying God because our assumed purpose for life is being blocked. How can we possibly glorify God when we or our loved ones are not healthy, happy, fulfilled, and successful? But if we rightly move ourselves and our families from the center of the universe and understand that we all exist to cast the spotlight on how great and important God is, then we can continue to glorify God even when life hurts and our desires aren't satisfied.

The apostle Paul shows us this right perspective in a dramatic setting. As he sat in jail unjustly accused and faced a potential death sentence, he declared that it was his eager expectation and hope that he would glorify God and honor Christ "whether by life or by death" (Philippians 1:20). Imagine that. He purposed to show the surpassing importance of God by his courage and boldness even if they executed him! In the same way, when Job entered into the excruciating pain and sense of loss on the day all his children died, he revealed his life's ultimate goal and worshipped God amid his grief, saying, "The LORD gave, and the LORD has taken away; blessed be the name of the LORD" (Job 1:21).

Thinking and speaking like this is impossible when we wrongly assume that the purpose of life is avoiding pain. It's possible only when we realize the point of life is to make sure that our words and our lives declare the exceeding importance of God and his incomparable worth. If that is your heart's desire, then much of what is to come, both in this chapter and the remainder of this book, will provide practical ways you can make this happen—even if your problem or pain doesn't go away.

Called to Be Obedient

When Daniel's three friends—Shadrach, Meshach, and Abednego—were told by their Babylonian captors to bow down and worship a gold image, they kept firmly in mind one of the primary ways the Bible tells us our lives bring glory to God. They knew, no matter what, that they were called to be obedient. God had given them, as he has given us, a set of important commands that were to demonstrate their love and fidelity to God. The New Testament expresses it this way:

> As obedient children, do not be conformed to the passions of your former ignorance, but as he who called

you is holy, you also be holy in all your conduct (1 Peter 1:14-15).

This is a life goal, which the Bible repeatedly shows us can be accomplished both when life is good and when life hurts. For Shadrach, Meshach, and Abednego, had "avoiding the pain" been their goal instead of obedience, we probably wouldn't even know their names. As prisoners of war, these three young men could have complained about their troubled lives and their loss of freedom. They could have said, "Why cause more trouble for ourselves? Why not just go with the flow? While in Babylon, let's just do as the Babylonians do!" But instead, they said:

> O Nebuchadnezzar, we have no need to answer you in this matter. If this be so, our God whom we serve is able to deliver us from the burning fiery furnace, and he will deliver us out of your hand, O king. But if not, be it known to you, O king, that we will not serve your gods or worship the golden image that you have set up (Daniel 3:16-18).

Did you catch the key phrase? They said, "But if not..." Their commitment to obey God and do as he commanded was not dependent on God delivering them. They knew God was able. And they hoped that he would. "But if not," they were going to obey him anyway. That was what they were called by God to do, and they intended to glorify him by obeying him no matter what.

God has commanded you and I not to fret, not to doubt his love, not to complain, and instead, to praise him and be thankful, among other things. When my daughter was initially diagnosed with her life-threatening condition, I knew God was able to deliver her. I prayed that he would. At the same time, I had to resist the temptation to fret and complain—even if things never got better. I was called to glorify God with an obedient life, which included offering up praise and thanksgiving to him no matter what.

When life gets difficult, we can easily give up and live like the Babylonians, bowing down to fear, worry, doubt, and bitterness. But we bring God glory when we purpose, as those three Jewish prisoners did, to obey his commands whether he delivers us from our crisis or not.

We have no record of Shadrach, Meshach, and Abednego ever being allowed to return to their homes in Israel. But we do know that God graciously delivered them from the fiery penalty of not bowing down to the Babylonian idol. Sometimes God does that. And it is in those times that these predicaments feel like tests. Often they are. Will we obey God amid the pain? Will we do what we know we should? But sometimes the painful trials are not being used by God to test us. Instead, it is not uncommon that the fiery pain itself is God's tool to refine us and make us more obedient than we were before.

Consider Paul's chronic medical problem, which he called his "thorn" (2 Corinthians 12:1-10). Paul pleaded three times for this to be removed. When God did not take the thorn away, Paul began to realize that God was using the pain itself to drive him to be more humble, more reliant on God, and more confident in God's good plan for his life and ministry. For Paul the uncomfortable ailment was more than the context for obedience. Rather, it became a catalyst for greater obedience.

So before you dejectedly cry out, "Why is this happening to me?" be sure you ask yourself, "How can I bring glory to God by being obedient in the middle of this crisis?" Then take it a step further and think, *How might this painful season be used as a springboard for less sin and greater obedience in my life?*

Called to Prove my Faith

One of the many misconceptions about Christianity is that the endgame for us is some translucent experience as disembodied spirits floating through eternity on cotton-ball clouds. However, the truth is that God is preparing for us a very real and tangible place to live, and each of us will be given a perfect body impervious to sickness, disease, and death. We will live and enjoy good food, friends, fellowship, and adventures that are yet to be revealed. But for now, as the Bible says, "we see in a mirror dimly, but then face to face" (1 Corinthians 13:12). "What we will be has not yet appeared; but we know that when he appears we shall be like him, because we shall see him as he is" (1 John 3:2). For today we are called to "walk by faith, not by sight" (2 Corinthians 5:7).

> The painful situations you experience are designed by God as opportunities for you to prove your faith.

God wants us to glorify him by keeping our faith strong regardless of our circumstances. He wants us to move through this life toward the next one with a confident trust in his good promises. See how it is stated in 1 Peter 1:

> Blessed be the God and Father of our Lord Jesus Christ! According to his great mercy, he has caused us to be born again to a living hope through the resurrection of Jesus Christ from the dead, to an inheritance that is imperishable, undefiled, and unfading, kept in heaven for you, who by God's power are being guarded through faith for a salvation ready to be revealed in the last time. In this you rejoice, though now for a little while, if necessary, you have been grieved by various trials, so that the tested genuineness of your faith—more precious than gold that perishes though it is tested by fire—may be found to result in praise and glory and honor at the revelation of Jesus Christ. Though you have not seen him, you love him. Though you do not now see him, you believe in him and rejoice with joy that is inexpressible and filled with glory (1 Peter 1:3-8).

As schoolchildren we all dreaded the tests handed out by our teachers. In fact, most of us hated them. Especially the hard ones that really probed the depths of what we had (or hadn't) studied. It's worth noting that the word God uses, and the word that has become synonymous with painful situations in the Christian life, is "trials"—literally, "tests." As 1 Peter 1 points out, these trials cause us grief. They are equated with fire. But in the end, when we pass them, they "result in praise and glory and honor" as we finally see Christ face to face.

The painful situations you experience are designed by God as opportunities for you to prove your faith—to prove that you really believe what you say you know to be true. How you handle life's difficulties will either confirm your trust in God and his promise of a future "inheritance" which is "imperishable, undefiled, and unfading, kept in heaven for you," or it will reveal that you don't really believe any of that.

While many of today's false teachers tell us that our ultimate happiness and fulfillment is intended to be "here and now," the Bible regularly reminds us that the ultimate hope of the Christian life is actually scheduled for the "then and there." Biblical Christianity has always instructed us to pin our hopes on our coming inheritance in the next life. Jesus plainly said, "In the world you will have tribulation. But take heart; I have overcome the world" (John 16:33). The apostles regularly preached that "through many tribulations we must enter the kingdom of God" (Acts 14:22). Jesus said that some people superficially attached themselves to him, but "when tribulation or persecution arises," they "immediately" fall away (Matthew 13:21).

Real faith doesn't fail, even when it is put under pressure. Real faith, even amid the pain, can say, "God is good." "The best is yet to come." "God is still God, and we will continue to love and follow Christ, come what may." And that doesn't mean we are joyless here and now. On the contrary, when we affirm our faith in God's good promises and continue to love and believe Christ, as 1 Peter 1:8 puts it, we can sincerely "rejoice with joy that is inexpressible and filled with glory."

Called to Be Spiritually Mature

How often, under the mounting pressure of another difficult test at school, have students complained, "Why am I doing this? I will never use this information in real life!" Often they are right. The minutiae on the upcoming calculus exam may never be used in the life of a firefighter or a dance instructor. But, as parents have said countless times to their discouraged teenagers, "The experience of hard work and study required for this difficult exam is preparing you for your line of work, whatever that might be."

Part of the focus we need to maintain as we seek to tenaciously trust in a good God in the middle of bad times is that God is working in us to strengthen and mature us. Getting us to endure pain with a right perspective is part of God's way of spiritually developing us. It is his way of getting us ready for a variety of things that he may be preparing us to do. The Bible says this is one reason we should "rejoice in our sufferings, knowing that suffering produces endurance, and endurance produces character, and character produces hope" (Romans 5:3-4).

> God uses our painful circumstances to make us more useful for his purposes in this world.

Don't underestimate how useful this kind of mature endurance, character, and hope will be for what God wants to do through you in this world. How hopeful are you in evangelism? How strong is your character when you face temptation? How resolutely do you endure in doing good? At first it may be hard to see the value of a health crisis or a financial collapse in terms of winning a neighbor to Christ, marital fidelity, or being a true blessing in someone's life. But the connections exist.

God uses our painful circumstances to make us more useful for his purposes in this world. I can't help but say to a Christian friend who has landed on hard times, "Welcome to seminary!" I know that as a growing Christian, my friend wants to be useful to God and the advancement of his work. I want him to know that the painful "tests" are precisely what the Lord will use to mature and prepare him for greater productivity and more effective ministry. The Bible couldn't be clearer about the way God uses trials in our lives:

> Count it all joy, my brothers, when you meet trials of various kinds, for you know that the testing of your faith produces steadfastness. And let steadfastness have its full effect, that you may be perfect and complete, lacking in nothing (James 1:2-4).

Initially you may find it impossible to truly "count it all joy." But think for a moment how being mindful of God's purpose behind the pain may actually help transform your attitude about it.

Ask any high school football player. Or better yet, listen to the way they talk after the grueling August practices just before the season starts. Sure, they talk about the pain, but they also exhibit an almost palpable pride and honor from having endured through those painful practices. They understand where those arduous experiences will take them. They look to their hard-fought spot on the team. They keep in view their hopes of a winning season. They know that the pain has a purpose—one for which they are very excited. They know that their struggle is making them stronger, better, and more useful to the coach.

Our Supreme Goals

Maturing Christians want nothing more than to bring glory to God. We want to obey Christ even when times are tough. We want an increasing confidence that today's pain in no way threatens the good promises of our future inheritance. We want our present trials to make us stronger and even more useful to the Master.

Keeping these supreme goals in view changes everything. Especially when our prayers for relief are not immediately answered. These goals can and should quickly become the focus of our prayers. I invite you to pray, as so many did with Carlynn and me during our toughest trials: *"Lord, as long as this problem or pain persists, let me look for ways to bring glory to you. May I seek to always obey you, to always increase my faith, and to always grow and mature as your servant."*

Chapter 4

Rethinking Fairness

I t's not fair!"

Who hasn't, at some painful low point in life, blurted out these words? It's easy to do. We only have to look around and notice that someone "worse" than us is having a "better" life. When our daughter was diagnosed with her serious birth defect, it didn't take long for some people to look at us with sympathy and say, "And you, being in the ministry and all." The assumption was that because we had given our lives to serve the Lord and to help people, it just wasn't fair that such "good people" would have such a "bad thing" happen to their little girl.

As the massive popularity of Rabbi Harold Kushner's book *When Bad Things Happen to Good People* [1] can attest, people desperately want an answer to this nagging concern. And while I can readily sympathize with the pain caused by the disease and subsequent death of Kushner's young son, which prompted his book, I cannot agree with his unbiblical answers. These bad events were not beyond God's control, as Kushner suggests. And our sovereign God has given us answers for the presence of evil in our world. Unfortunately, most people don't care to hear them.

If we are going to grapple with the question of "bad things" hap-pening to "good people," we have to be careful to understand the question in two distinct ways. As I've hinted by my repeated use of quotation marks around "good people" and "bad things," we have to realize that there is both an absolute way as well as a relative way to consider this question. In other words, we have to realize that when we talk about "good people," we usually don't mean *abso-lutely* good. And when we talk about "bad things," we usually don't mean *ultimately* and *eternally* bad things. But to think rightly about this tough question, and our own suffering, we really need to think through this distinction.

Relative vs. Absolute

When the rich young ruler came to Jesus to ask him how he could inherit eternal life, the ruler addressed Jesus by calling him, "Good Teacher" (Luke 18:18). Jesus' response was intended to make the young man rethink the person to whom he was speaking. Christ said, "Why do you call me good? No one is good except God alone" (verse 19). In saying this, Jesus was calling attention to the exclu-sive, absolute goodness of God. Only God is perfectly holy. Only God is absolutely righteous. And only God is *absolutely* and *truly* good. Everyone else, the Bible says, is sinful. All human beings have "sinned and fall short of the glory of God" (Romans 3:23).

If we contemplate the exacting standards of God's moral law, which reflect His perfect character, it shouldn't take long for us to admit that we are all sinners. Relatively speaking, we are not all the same kind of sinners. Some people sin more and some sin worse than others. So some people may be more "good" than others. But for now, let's consider the age-old question in the absolute sense of the word *good*. Why do bad things happen to good (as in truly good) people? The answer is, they don't.

That may not be a satisfying answer. And for some it may sound like an insensitive and even offensive answer. But it is the right answer—at least in an absolute sense. Instead, we could ask the question this way: Why do bad things happen to sinners? But a title like that probably wouldn't make it on the *New York Times* best-seller list.

Consider also that we usually aren't talking about absolutely and eternally bad things. Painful? Yes. Absolutely bad? Not usually. When we speak of "bad things" happening, we are usually referring to difficult trials, pain, disease, and even biological death. Only in some cases are we talking about the absolute reality of being eternally lost. But for Christians, being lost eternally will never happen. God's children are promised that when they die they will never hear "I never knew you; depart from me" (Matthew 7:23). Because of Christ's life, death, and resurrection, those of us who trust in him for forgiveness have been assured that we will never incur the eternal punishment our sins deserve. Instead, we will be ushered into eternal life (Matthew 25:46). So if you are asking, "Why do bad [as in eternally bad] things happen to Christians?" The answer again is, they don't!

> Any true understanding of God's fairness has to begin with a biblical discussion of sin.

But that may bring little comfort when you've been diagnosed with cancer, have to endure chronic pain, or have just lost everything financially. However, rightly pondered, this truth should probably bring us more comfort than it does. Paul wrote about some painful "bad things" in his life (things most of us wouldn't want to trade for ours) and referred to them as "light momentary affliction." Why? Because he was looking "not to the things that are seen but to the things that are unseen," knowing that "the things that are seen are transient, but the things that are unseen are eternal" (2 Corinthians 4:17-18).

Absolute Fairness

Any true understanding of God's fairness has to begin with a biblical discussion of sin. To help us, let's imagine a group of skunks. Let's suppose there are a few skunks in the group that the rest of the skunks consider stinky. You might reasonably claim that the accusing skunks are hypocrites. But that, of course, is based on your human perspective. We humans consider all skunks stinky. But from the group's perspective, their claim is valid. "The stinky skunks," they insist, "are truly stinky, not us!" These "average skunks" can tolerate the smell of the other average skunks, and of course themselves, but they cannot tolerate those whom they consider to be "really stinky."

The problem with all of our discussions about God's fairness is that we struggle with our perception of who is and who isn't a sinner—who "stinks" and who doesn't. As I quoted earlier, "all have sinned and fall short of the glory of God" (Romans 3:23). In other words, measured by God's holy standard, we all stink—we are all sinners. Sure, we can point to those who "really stink," but that assessment is made from our perspective, not God's. This doesn't mean that God doesn't perceive the difference between the stinky and the really stinky, but that also doesn't change the reality that to a holy and perfect God we are all sinners.

There is something else we need to rightly understand before we consider the question of God's fairness—namely, God's goodness. To help us with this concept, let's imagine my backyard. In my yard I have a large hedge that shrouds our back fence, which borders some undeveloped open space. Unfortunately, my thick green hedge is an irresistible lodging place for the rats that scavenge all night out in the adjacent field. As you can imagine, it's unnerving to hear these creepy little rodents scurrying around in the hedge when I walk out into my backyard. Over the years, I've worked to exterminate these disease-infested pests. And my intermittent success is cheered on by my family, guests, and neighbors. But suppose for a minute that I choose to adopt a couple of the hedge rats. Imagine that one afternoon I carefully pluck them from the hedge. I give them their needed vaccinations, thoroughly clean them up, and buy them little blue and pink collars. And I decide to call one Rita and one Randy. I then gift Rita and Randy to my son, who generously feeds them, plays with them, and lovingly cares for them. (As you know, such acts of kindness toward rodents are not all that uncommon these days.) What could be said against my discriminating actions toward rats? Some I exterminate, and others I adopt, shower with gifts, and envelop in my son's love and care. It is certainly my right to do as I choose—considering that they were all disease-infested rodents to begin with, and I am the sovereign property owner.

While such a bold illustration might not inflate our self-esteem, it does reveal something of the biblical picture of God's goodness. The good things that the Owner of all things chooses to do for sinful people flow from the undeserved kindness of the Giver, not the intrinsic worth or lovability of the ones who receive his good gifts. Considering what the holy and sinless God should *justly* give to repulsive skunks or creepy rodents helps us to understand that all of God's good gifts are truly gravy. Absolute fairness gives nothing good to sinful men and women. The amazing realization is not "Why don't all the rodents have nice sweaters?" but "Why do any rodents have sweaters at all?" The amazing thing isn't that the homeowner is repelled by the rats; instead, the amazing thing is "grace…that saved a wretch like me."

If we can begin to understand who we really are in relation to a sinless God, and if we can agree that any good thing that we fallen humans experience is an undeserved gift (no matter how superior we may feel compared to another fallen human), then perhaps we can realize that the real question isn't "Why has this bad thing happened to me?" but "Why have I ever experienced any good things?" In other words, we need to stop saying we want fairness. Instead, we need to celebrate that God is incredibly gracious.

Job's View of Fairness

Watch this rare perspective in action—when in a single day natural disasters and a band of criminals decimated Job's life savings. Worse still, a windstorm collapsed his oldest son's house, killing his son and the rest of Job's ten children. Remarkably, Job responded by saying,

> "Naked I came from my mother's womb, and naked shall
> I return. The LORD gave, and the LORD has taken away;
> blessed be the name of the LORD." In all this Job did not
> sin or charge God with wrong (Job 1:21-22).

Job didn't say, "God, it was unfair of you to take away the children whom I loved and the wealth that I enjoyed." Instead, he blessed God for having graciously given him the things he loved and previously enjoyed. Job understood the undeserved kindness he had received in the gift of children and wealth. He knew he deserved none of these good gifts from God. He saw that when it came to absolute fairness, it was unfair for him to have experienced any of those good years with his beloved children or any of the blessings of wealth.

While I may have called this a "rare perspective" and a "remarkable" response, look again at how the inspired writer of Job commented on this response. He said, "Job did not sin or charge God with wrong" (verse 22). God's Word affirms that this was the right response—a response that shouldn't be rare among God's people. In fact, the Bible groups the charging of God with wrong for taking away these loving relations and hard-earned assets with sin. We have become conditioned by our lost world to shake our fist at God. We gladly accept the truckloads of undeserved gifts from God, but once we learn to love them or enjoy them, we evidently believe he has no right to take these undeserved gifts away.

Unfortunately as Job's grief wore on, and after the bad counsel of his friends saturated his conversations, his godly perspective waned. Much of the book of Job shows us Job's retreat into a kind of smug and frustrated claim of injustice at his loss. But the last two conversations Job has—one with Elihu and the other with God himself (Job 32–42)—are recorded to show us that Job had gotten things grossly out of perspective, and that he actually had it right in the first chapter.

In the midst of his grief and pain, Job needed to stop thinking that he deserved good gifts from God and had some right or claim to them because he "was better" than the next guy. As Elihu put it, "If you are righteous, what do you give to him? Or what does he receive from your hand?" (Job 35:7). There was no "absolute fairness" in all the good things Job had received. Ultimately, they were all undeserved and unearned gifts from God. They were not the fair and equitable payback for him "measuring up" to God's perfect standard of holiness.

God Is Gracious

God's generous grace is the theme of the closing chapters of Job. In those chapters, God illustrates over and over again that he is the merciful Provider of all good things. All life has been granted by him. He made and sustains all things. He gives stars their light and the oceans their limits. He sends his rains and causes the earth to produce its crops. He graciously satisfies the hunger of the animals of the forests, and he enables flight to all the birds of the sky. The stars don't earn their light and the birds don't bargain for their talents. God has graciously given all things. These gifts are his merciful prerogative. He can do as he pleases with his gifts. And he can grant them as he chooses.

God also reminded Job that he, a frail human, had no power or authority to control the peoples of the earth, let alone control God. Job could not direct the eating patterns of the wild animals, nor could he pacify the strength of the massive beasts of the field. With such little strength, what a foolish thing it was for him to think that he could control, contain, or domesticate the God who made all things.

Comprehending more clearly the grace of Almighty God, Job confessed:

> I know that you can do all things, and that no purpose
> of yours can be thwarted…Therefore I have uttered
> what I did not understand, things too wonderful for me,
> which I did not know…therefore I despise myself, and
> repent…(Job 42:2-3,6).

Perhaps before we go any further we should do the same. We
have all been tempted to reach that point in our suffering where we
begin to question God's goodness, his fairness, or his wisdom. We
are tempted to speak as though God were on trial and we, his accus-
ers, had the rights to all his good gifts and blessings. So if we, like
Job, have fallen to this temptation, it is time for us to admit that we
have been lulled into a wrong view of God. We should confess that
we have said things about our situation that we really don't understand. We should repent and humbly ask God for his most needed
blessing—his forgiveness.

Thankfully, God is extraordinarily generous with his grace of forgiveness. The book of Job ends by showing us the Lord's merciful
pardon and restoration of Job. After his terrible season of excruciating pain and suffering, Job is comforted and restored by God. Job's
foolish words and misguided rants are forgiven. He comes through
this trial having stumbled, but ultimately refined and reeducated
about God's amazing grace.

Relative Fairness

While we are wise to never want God's "absolute fairness," there
are many godly people like Job who have struggled with the way
God distributes his blessings and gifts. It's true that no sinner
deserves health and wealth, but the reality is that all kinds of sinners
have them—and to our annoyance, it seems that often some of the
worst sinners have a lot more of them than we do.

Even when we affirm that none of us deserve any of God's gracious blessings, it is still profoundly painful for a Christian couple to
suffer with infertility while our society is filled with teen pregnancies

and abortions. And it is distressing when Christians in the prime of their lives are diagnosed with cancer while godless people down the street grow old in excellent health. There is no doubt that lost jobs, foreclosed homes, failed marriages, being the victim of a crime, and the death of loved ones are made even more difficult for us when we see that remarkably sinful people are lavished with God's good gifts.

When our daughter was finally born, she was immediately whisked off to what the doctors informed us would likely be the first in a series of major surgeries. Down the hall in the waiting room our family and friends were anxiously anticipating news on how Stephanie was, and whether this critical surgery would be successful. The mood was tense. In stark contrast, there were several sets of families and friends in the large hospital waiting with balloons and gifts for the delivery of healthy babies who were soon to be celebrated and embraced. There the mood was joyful and expectant.

It was a difficult day for many of our friends and family members. Those who admired our lives and ministry also struggled with the further comparison that many of the healthy children born in that hospital, along with the thousands born in hospitals across the country, were being born to people who, to put it nicely, were not so admirable. The thought of perfectly healthy babies being born to those who were shamelessly opposed to what was good, while a pastor and his wife were having to roll their newborn into the operating room, was "not right."

There is no avoiding these kinds of comparisons in life. They are the kinds of real-life contrasts that make us frustrated or mad, and often tempt us to accuse God of doing something wrong. These types of thoughts may have crossed your mind and may have even come out of your mouth. They were certainly the kinds of thoughts that dragged Job into a bad mental state from which he later had to repent.

And Job is not the only godly person in the Bible who voiced such frustrations. In Psalm 73, one of King David's worship leaders, named Asaph, confessed that he was envious when he "saw the prosperity of the wicked" (verse 3). He resentfully recounted all the good things they experienced—their good fortune, the abundance of their income, their good health—and then bemoaned that his "clean" life had been rewarded with nothing but trouble and opposition day after day (verse 13).

Often our frustration is compounded by the fact that the Bible repeatedly tells us that good behavior is rewarded and sinful behavior brings adverse consequences. Imagine Asaph pondering the lyrics that open Israel's song book:

> Blessed is the man who walks not in the counsel of the wicked, nor stands in the way of sinners, nor sits in the seat of scoffers; but his delight is in the law of the LORD, and on his law he meditates day and night. He is like a tree planted by streams of water that yields its fruit in its season, and its leaf does not wither. In all that he does, he prospers. The wicked are not so, but are like chaff that the wind drives away. Therefore the wicked will not stand in the judgment, nor sinners in the congregation of the righteous; for the LORD knows the way of the righteous, but the way of the wicked will perish (Psalm 1).

It couldn't be clearer. The good guys are supposed to prosper, and the sinners are supposed to be punished. Asaph was struggling. Something was not right.

When Inequities Make You Feel Like Giving Up

In Psalm 73, Asaph confessed that because of the perceived inequities of life he felt like giving up. Maybe trusting God, doing good, and following God's path in life weren't worth it after all. He poetically wrote,

> All in vain have I kept my heart clean and washed my hands in innocence. For all the day long I have been stricken and rebuked every morning (Psalm 73:13-14).

On bad days we'll be tempted to feel just like that. Amid our crushing pain and disappointment our emotions will cry out, "What's the point? Does all my investment in seeking God, trusting Christ, and doing the right thing really pay off?"

King David knew this pain all too well. Consider that after the prophet Samuel came and ceremonially anointed this inexperienced shepherd boy as the next king of Israel, David rose up in faith and boldly killed the Philistine giant, Goliath. You would think that the red carpet to the throne of Israel would be rolled out immediately. But it wasn't. In fact, we read in the very next chapter of the Bible that the outgoing King Saul would have nothing of it. Saul turned on the one who was said to be loved and chosen by God. He began years of opposition and attack against the young would-be king.

David spent years living in caves in the desert. He even had to live in enemy territory and wondered if stepping up to follow God's path for his life was worth it. In trying to serve the nation, it appeared as though everyone had turned against him. Hadn't he been better off when he was watching his father's sheep? Now, having trusted God, he had walked into a war zone. Read the pain-filled words of one of the psalms David wrote and sympathize with him as he runs from Saul and his armies, who sought to destroy his life.

> ...without cause they hid their net for me; without cause
> they dug a pit for my life...Malicious witnesses rise up;
> they ask me of things that I do not know. They repay me
> evil for good; my soul is bereft...at my stumbling they
> rejoiced and gathered; they gathered together against
> me; wretches whom I did not know tore at me with-
> out ceasing; like profane mockers at a feast, they gnash
> at me with their teeth. How long, O Lord, will you look
> on?...They open wide their mouths against me...You
> have seen, O LORD; be not silent! O Lord, be not far
> from me! Awake and rouse yourself for my vindication
> (Psalm 35:7, 11-12, 15-17, 21-23).

Here we have the heart of a man who was told that he was highly favored and deeply loved by God. But life sure didn't feel that way! At least not during this chapter of David's life. There may be a hint of hope in these cries, but there is also plenty of hurt and a clear feeling of abandonment. How long, O Lord? You see my pain. You know this isn't right. Where are you? When will you step in with your help and vindication?

While David waited fifteen long and tumultuous years for God to change his circumstances, he often wrote of how God was at work in his heart. Even at some of his lowest points David wrote songs that expressed the way God was supporting him during these painful seasons. While he hid in desert caves to protect his life, David said to the Lord, "In you my soul takes refuge; in the shadow of your wings I will take refuge, till the storms of destruction pass by" (Psalm 57:1).

What a vivid picture of David's trust in God's care! Yes, I'm on the run. Sure, it's not right. Yes, I've been betrayed by people whom I've been good to. But God will get me through this. I will look to him. I will continue to trust him. I know in time this storm will pass.

In faith, David wrote,

> I cry out to God Most High, to God who fulfills his purpose for me. He will send from heaven and save me; he will put to shame him who tramples on me. God will send out his steadfast love and his faithfulness! My soul is in the midst of lions; I lie down amid fiery beasts—the children of man, whose teeth are spears and arrows, whose tongues are sharp swords. Be exalted, O God, above the heavens! Let your glory be over all the earth!…My heart is steadfast, O God, my heart is steadfast! I will sing and make melody! Awake, my glory! Awake, O harp and lyre! I will awake the dawn! (Psalm 57:2-5, 7-8).

David resolved to "settle in with God" for the duration. I will trust God. He will get me through it. I will purpose to praise him, and I will crank up the volume on my praise.

Though the Bible doesn't describe the setting in which David penned his most familiar psalm, Psalm 23, the words certainly reflect the threat and danger of when he was running for his life:

> Even though I walk through the valley of the shadow of death, I will fear no evil, for you are with me; your rod and your staff, they comfort me. You prepare a table before me in the presence of my enemies; you anoint my head with oil; my cup overflows. Surely goodness and mercy shall follow me all the days of my life, and I shall dwell in the house of the LORD forever (Psalm 23:4-6).

In the trying times David experienced, he learned to cultivate an intimate spiritual connection with God. It is as though his circumstances faded to the background as he focused on his relationship with the Lord, which was all that really mattered. David's spirit was sustained and his faith bolstered when he reached out to his Shepherd, who calmed his heart—even when the valley grew darker and threatened his very life.

Acknowledging God's Care

Both David and Asaph could have kept their focus on how "unfair" it was that they were doing right and yet everything seemed to be going wrong. But they didn't. Even in their darkest hours, these men were careful to acknowledge God's faithful provision. This is an important place for our minds and prayers to go when things in our lives seem unfair.

> Even in the deepest and darkest places of our lives, we need to step back and acknowledge God's present provisions.

David knew that, like a faithful shepherd, even when he was surrounded by enemies or in the deepest valleys, God was providing for him in a variety of ways. His basic needs were being met, and plenty of "good and perfect gifts" continued to flow from God (see James 1:17). And after all the pains and inequities that Asaph endured, he wrote, "Nevertheless, I am continually with you; you hold my right hand" (Psalm 73:23).

Even in the deepest and darkest places of our lives, we need to step back and acknowledge God's present provisions. Like children who are quick to lose perspective, we need to remember with whom we are walking through this painful journey.

Though in our crisis regarding our newborn daughter Carlynn and I could have made a long list of the things that were going wrong, instead we purposed to stop frequently to acknowledge God's kind and generous hand of provision. We had decent medical insurance. We had good prenatal care. Our daughter had well-trained surgeons at the ready. We had a church family who cared and prayed for us. We had each other. We had a roof over our heads. We had more than enough of life's necessities. We had two other children, for whose good health we now thanked God more than ever. God had been and was continuing to be generous and kind to the Fabarez family, even as we faced the darkest valley that our family had ever faced.

The saying "Count your blessings" may seem old and trite. But there's no better time to do this than when you face life's trials. Ask yourself: What are some of the signs of God's daily provision? How is God's generous hand still evident in your crisis? What are the things for which you can now be thankful? "Awake [the] harp," as David wrote, and express your praise and thanksgiving to God— even as you lay your burdened requests before him.

Few knew it better than David: "The Lord is a stronghold for the oppressed, a stronghold in times of trouble. And those who know your name put their trust in you, for you, O LORD, have not forsaken those who seek you" (Psalm 9:9).

Thanking God for his provision in the midst of life's "unfair" storms can be comforting. But to discover a deep and abiding sense of peace when life is tough, we need what Job, David, and Asaph all eventually learned and had—we need to have a much bigger perspective. As we will discover, God has a lot to say about straining our vision beyond this world's horizon.

CHAPTER 5

Why Being Heavenly Minded
Does a World of Good

Like most artists, M.C. Escher, the twentieth-century Dutch graphic artist, reflected something of his life experiences in his artwork. Escher initially studied to be an architect, but due to his recurring illnesses, he was unable to graduate from school. He moved to Rome in the 1920s, but had to flee when Mussolini launched his fascist regime. Later, Escher made his home in Belgium, but was again forced to flee as the chaos of World War II began. He eventually settled in the Netherlands, where his bad health, combined with the bad weather, made for a difficult final season of his life. Perhaps it is no surprise then that Escher became famous for his "not-quite-right" perspective drawings. In his artwork, things that ought to go up are portrayed as going down. Things that should be connected aren't. Parts of buildings that should be in the front cleverly and convincingly appear to be in the back. Paths that should be straight are bent. It is not hard to see how the not-how-it-ought-to-be realities that he vividly portrayed were an expression of his sad and turbulent life.

Every time I see one of M.C. Escher's perspective drawings I can't help but think of Isaiah's prophetic depiction of the current state of our world. Clearly things are not as they ought to be. Isaiah lamented about people who "call evil good and good evil," "put darkness for light and light for darkness," and substitute "bitter for sweet and sweet for bitter" (Isaiah 5:20). Later he wrote that far too often people's

> feet run to evil, and they are swift to shed innocent blood; their thoughts are thoughts of iniquity; desolation and destruction are in their highways. The way of peace they do not know, and there is no justice in their paths; they have made their roads crooked; no one who treads on them knows peace. Therefore justice is far from us, and righteousness does not overtake us; we hope for light, and behold, darkness, and for brightness, but we walk in gloom (Isaiah 59:7-9).

Especially during the difficult seasons of life, it is easy to see that this world is far from what it ought to be. We hope for a beautiful picture of how life ought to be, but regrettably, we catch only glimpses of it. Reality is not what we would hope. We thirst for a reality this present world cannot quench. As C.S. Lewis expressed, "If [we] find in [ourselves] a desire which no experience in this world can satisfy, the most probable explanation is that [we] were made for another world."[1] That is clearly the message of the Bible. And as Christians we can confidently say that we were made—or more accurately, "remade"—for another world. God transformed our hearts the moment we repented and placed our faith in Christ. We now have a real relational connection to the perfect God, and our hearts rightly long for the reality that Isaiah tried to get his readers' hearts fixed on. One in which "every valley shall be exalted and every mountain and hill brought low; the crooked places shall be made straight and the rough places smooth" (Isaiah 40:4 NKJV).

When we suffer, it is important that we affirm two very important truths. First, we must remember that God has made clear that for now things on this planet are certainly not as they ought to be. And second, we must confidently rest in the prom- ise that, for God's people, one day they will be! Being honest about the first, and setting our sights on the second, will radically transform almost everything about our attitude, per- spective, and disposition as we work our way through the dark valleys of suffering and pain.

> It is only a matter of timing. God *will* right all wrongs and rectify every painful problem for his people.

Seeing the Big Picture

When Asaph was overwhelmed by the pain of his circumstances and found himself envying the wicked, who seemed to be enjoying a much better life than he was, he confessed that he struggled to make sense of it all. That is, until he was challenged to get a bigger perspective. He wrote:

> When I thought how to understand this, it seemed to me a wearisome task, until I went into the sanctuary of God; then I discerned their end. Truly you set them in slippery places; you make them fall to ruin. How they are destroyed in a moment, swept away utterly by terrors!...You guide me with your counsel, and afterward you will receive me to glory. Whom have I in heaven but you? And there is nothing on earth that I desire besides you (Psalm 73:16-18, 24-25).

A trip to "church" helped Asaph remember that the present injustice—of the wicked prospering and God's people being plagued with pain and suffering—was only a temporary situation. The biblical declaration that God's people will prosper and that the wicked will be driven away like the chaff in the wind is true (Psalm 1:3-4). Any evidence to the contrary is short-lived. It is only a matter of timing. God *will* right all wrongs and rectify every painful problem for his people. Of course, we naturally want the fix now, and at times we do see God graciously provide some fixes. But all the permanent fixes are certain and forthcoming with the promised arrival of Christ's kingdom.

The Good of Our Future Good

Getting our pain in perspective begins by affirming that while bad is certainly bad, it is not as bad as our future good is good. Did you follow that? In other words, the eternal absolute perfection of the good that God has planned for his people cannot reasonably be compared to the various shades of temporary pain and suffering we now experience. That's the point Paul was trying to express when he wrote, "I consider that the sufferings of this present time are not worth comparing with the glory that is to be revealed to us" (Romans 8:18).

We always endure pain much more tenaciously when we know that there is an end in sight—especially when we anticipate that there will be a gratifying payoff when we reach the light at the end of the tunnel. This reminds me of my dad's recent knee replacement. Not an exciting prospect on the surface of things. No one arbitrarily wants to sign up for knee surgery. Not to mention the painful physical therapy that follows.

Like many knee-replacement patients, my father needed both knees replaced. Because of the inherent risks, the doctor would not agree to do them both at the same time. So after the discomfort of one surgery, the woozy recovery, and the excruciating pain of physical therapy, the doctor came to my dad and said, "Okay, let's replace the other one." For my father, the prospect of another round of throbbing pain, hospital food, and the unyielding therapist was overshadowed by the hope of a new knee that promised to work as knees were intended to work.

It was easier for my dad to sign up for the second surgery having experienced the initial benefits of the first surgery. One knee had been fixed, giving him the ability to imagine just how good it would be to have them both fixed. That's a lot like the reality we face as Christians. At our conversion, many things change for the better. We are graciously allowed to experience a profound fix in our relationship with God. The Bible calls this reconciliation, and it changes everything about the way we know and relate to our Maker. We are also given a permanent connection with God's Spirit. The Holy Spirit invades our lives—bringing forgiveness and eradicating our guilt. As the New Testament writers put it, we have "tasted" the goodness of God (1 Peter 2:3) because we have "the firstfruits of the Spirit" (Romans 8:23).

But as these phrases suggest, this is just the beginning. There is much more to come. It is good to know God in this life, but there is much more to the "fix" provided by the salvation we have in Christ. John wrote: "We are God's children now, and what we will be has not yet appeared; but we know that when he appears we shall be like him" (1 John 3:2). Paul said: "Now we see in a mirror dimly, but then face to face. Now I know in part; then I shall know fully" (1 Corinthians 13:12). Later Paul drove the point home by asserting that "if in Christ we have hope in this life only, we are of all people most to be pitied" (1 Corinthians 15:19).

Take a minute to slowly read about your certain future. You will see that everything that's wrong with this world will, by God's grace, be transformed into what it ought to be:

> I saw a new heaven and a new earth, for the first heaven and the first earth had passed away, and the sea was no more. And I saw the holy city, new Jerusalem, coming down out of heaven from God, prepared as a bride adorned for her husband. And I heard a loud voice from the throne saying, "Behold, the dwelling place of God is with man. He will dwell with them, and they will be his people, and God himself will be with them as their God. He will wipe away every tear from their eyes, and death shall be no more, neither shall there be mourning, nor

crying, nor pain anymore, for the former things have passed away."

And he who was seated on the throne said, "Behold, I am making all things new." Also he said, "Write this down, for these words are trustworthy and true." And he said to me, "It is done! I am the Alpha and the Omega, the beginning and the end. To the thirsty I will give from the spring of the water of life without payment" (Revelation 21:1-6).

Fixed Bodies

Going back to knee replacements, our bodies are going to need a lot more than a couple of new knees. The judgment that God imposed on a sinful world in Genesis 3 was that, for now, we'd be trapped in deteriorating bodies that would be subject to sickness, disease, congenital birth defects, rebellious cancer cells, and eventually, death. Much of life's suffering is related in one way or another to humanity's vulnerability to sickness, disease, and death. The good news is that Christ's death purchased for us, his followers, the benefit of a remanufactured physical body that will take our DNA back to the original Manufacturer's specifications. Here is how the Bible describes our new resurrection body in 1 Corinthians 15:42-44.

1. Ageless

Much like the produce items in the supermarket, the Bible characterizes our fallen bodies as "perishable" (verse 42). Not unlike the bananas on my kitchen counter, which seem to be "perfect" for only about a half a day, our physical bodies peak quickly and then start getting spotted and mushy before any of us want them to.

In the pattern of Jesus' resurrection, the Bible says that at his return God will take what's left of our decaying bodies and instantly reconstruct them in a way that will leave them impervious to decay.

First Corinthians 15:42 simply describes these remanufactured bodies as "imperishable." That means every fiber of our bodies will work as it was envisioned when God created the first human body. The elasticity of our skin will never age, sag, or wrinkle. Every follicle that was intended to produce rich, thick hair will; and every pore that wasn't, won't. And all the melanin, the proteins, and the enzymes will be perfectly regulated. Sound good? Christ's complete payment for sin on the cross has made this possible for us.

So if your current suffering stems from a failing, diseased, or broken body, take heart! As you pray for a fix, remember that all earthbound remedies are temporary. The real and ultimate hope is found at the end of road. God's permanent solution is a body that is eternally resistant to every illness, ailment, and affliction—forever!

2. Beautiful

Pondering the implications of an ageless body should make this next declaration easy to understand. First Corinthians 15 goes on to compare our present bodies with our future resurrected bodies by using the words "dishonor" and "glory" (verse 43). This present decaying body is increasingly dishonorable, but the remanufactured one will be characterized by glory. Earlier in his letter to the Corinthians, Paul used the word "dishonorable" to describe something that just didn't look right. And in this context, the word "glory" is used as it was in Christ's teaching about the lilies of the field when he said that "they neither toil nor spin, yet I tell you, even Solomon in all his glory was not arrayed like one of these" (Matthew 6:28-29).

Most of us would admit that at the peak of our growth and physical development we looked better than we do now. Some of us would say that even then, we weren't all that attractive. If that's the case, we can blame it on our imperfect genes. In the big scheme of things even the genetics of our family tree have been subject to decay. Maybe in your case the less-than-perfect biological data constructed a physical appearance that didn't come together the way you would have liked. Or, perhaps you would be happy for eternity looking the way you did when you were nineteen. Good for you, you likely will. Either way, the perfect and "glorious" expression of your uncorrupted DNA will be what you can expect when God transforms the "not-quite-right" version of what you're now living in.

3. Tireless

In the Garden of Gethsemane, before Christ's arrest and crucifixion, Jesus asked the disciples to pray with him. Yet they fell asleep. Jesus diagnosed their problem with the words, "The spirit indeed is willing, but the flesh is weak" (Matthew 26:41). This is certainly a problem on several levels. Our fallen bodies have so many limitations when it comes to strength, energy, and power. But according to God's promise in 1 Corinthians 15, the resurrected bodies that we will inhabit will no longer be characterized by weakness. Instead, they will be "raised in power" (verse 43). Sickness, disease, and the everyday process of growing older remind us all of how weak and frail our bodies really are. What a great expectation to know that God will one day encase our spirit in a body that has unlimited energy, vitality, and strength.

I've been tempted to wrongly envision the next life as an experience in which I get to sleep in all morning and nap all afternoon. But those desires stem from my present experience of growing weary and increasingly tired as the years roll by. The truth is our bodies won't need that kind of rest. Nor will they crave it. Consider the fact that in the last two chapters of the Bible, we are told twice that in the eternal home that God is preparing for us there will no longer be any nighttime (Revelation 21:25 and 22:5). That's certainly no "heaven" for fallen, tired, worn-out bodies, but for our new bodies with boundless energy it will be just perfect.

4. Godly

The last contrast listed in 1 Corinthians 15 is the difference between our current "natural" bodies and our remanufactured "spiritual" bodies (verse 44). Here's where many people go wrong in their expectations. It is easy to imagine "spiritual" as something ghostly, transparent, or nonphysical. That's why many people think that they will be see-through spirits in the next life, floating around endlessly on cotton-ball clouds. But that's not anything like Christ's resurrected body, which is said to be the prototype or "firstfruits" of our coming bodies (1 Corinthians 15:20, 23). Remember that Christ told his doubting disciples to reach out and touch him. And on more than one occasion he shared a meal with his disciples in his resurrected body (Luke 24:38-43; John 21:12-15).

Earlier, in 1 Corinthians chapter 2, Paul talked about the natural people and the spiritual people who made up the church at Corinth (1 Corinthians 2:15–3:1). He obviously didn't mean the see-through, ghostly, immaterial people as opposed to the physical people in the church. In much the same way we use the word today, Paul spoke of people who were "spiritual" and people who weren't. In other words, people who were directed and guided by God's Spirit—making good and godly choices, as compared to those who weren't.

Even in this life Christians talk about wanting to be more spiritual—meaning they want to be more in step with the Holy Spirit, growing and maturing in their walk with God. Here and now, this is only partial and incomplete. The good news is that our new body will always follow the directions of the Holy Spirit, and will always make good and godly choices. And in light of how much of our suffering in this life is related to the sinful and ungodly choices we and others make, this is a huge promise that should get us very excited for the next life.

Unparalleled Happiness

There is a powerful sentence—one that most people recognize more from Handel's Christmastime oratorio than they do from the Bible—which captures the seismic shift that will take place one day on God's prophetic calendar. It boldly states, "The kingdom of the world has become the kingdom of our Lord and of his Christ, and he shall reign forever and ever" (Revelation 11:15).

Imagine the implications of that promise! There will come a day when this will be the Lord God's world, and his ruling Messiah, Jesus Christ, will be the King. The Holy Spirit will indwell every citizen, and God will have his way. And everything he wants will be accomplished. Jesus will be the benevolent Leader whose good and perfect plans will always be carried out. Think about it—no need for governmental checks and balances, no opinion polls, no defiant protests, no rebellions, no insurrections, no crime, no corruption, and no misconduct. Instead, people who have been made perfect will be perfectly led by a perfect and unrivaled King.

> The bad we experience is inarguably bad, but it is not as bad as our future good is good.

The perfect goodness of our triune God will pervade this new society in every respect. All the inhabitants of this remade world will enjoy the unimaginable kindness and love of God himself. The good and perfect gifts of God will be generously bestowed on his children. The Bible says that in God's "presence there is fullness of joy; and at [his] right hand are pleasures forevermore" (Psalm 16:11). When Isaiah relayed God's surpassing promises about the forthcoming "new earth," he said that once we are established there it will be so good that "the former things shall not be remembered or come into mind" (Isaiah 65:17).

As I said earlier, the bad we experience is inarguably bad, but it is not as bad as our future good is good. Your future will be so amazing that looking back on this present reality will be a forgettable experience. Your present pain may be real and severe, but take heart; the future that God is planning for you is filled with incomparable happiness and joy.

Focused on Your Future

It is this eternal and glorious reality that should be our daily focus. Over and over again throughout the New Testament we are told in one way or another:

> If then you have been raised with Christ, seek the things that are above, where Christ is, seated at the right hand of God. Set your minds on things that are above, not on things that are on earth. For you have died, and your life is hidden with Christ in God. When Christ who is your life appears, then you also will appear with him in glory (Colossians 3:1-4).

The people of the world may mock us for what they consider a head-in-the-clouds mind-set, but don't let this rhetoric dissuade you. Oliver Wendell Holmes may have been known for saying, "Some people are so heavenly minded that they are no earthly good," but he was wrong. C.S. Lewis rightly countered, "It is since Christians have largely ceased to think of the other world that they have become so ineffective in this one. Aim at Heaven and you will get Earth 'thrown in': aim at Earth and you will get neither."[2]

This is certainly what the Bible teaches us, both in principle and by example. No one was more heavenly minded than Christ, and his life changed the world and the people in it more than any other in history. Certainly Peter, Paul, James, and John, just to mention a few, were continually telling us to get our minds on our future, imperishable, undefiled, and unfading inheritance (see 1 Peter 1:4-5). These were the kind of people who made a huge and lasting impact on this world for good.

It is not just your heart and your attitude that will be transformed when you fix your sight and your hope on the good God has in store for you in the next life; having this focus will also renovate the way you go about doing everything that you do. Your work, your conversation, your counsel, and your relationships will all be seasoned by the perspective and values of eternal things—things that truly matter. And as for getting your pain and suffering in perspective, nothing could be better. The Bible compares it to the tenacity and endurance that is demonstrated in the labor and delivery wings of hospitals everywhere. Paul said that the present pain, in light of the forthcoming joy, is like the perseverant groaning of a mother in the pains of childbirth (Romans 8:22-23). Jesus said,

> When a woman is giving birth, she has sorrow because her hour has come, but when she has delivered the baby, she no longer remembers the anguish, for joy that a human being has been born into the world. So also you have sorrow now, but I will see you again, and your hearts will rejoice, and no one will take your joy from you (John 16:21-22).

Given the pain and suffering involved in childbirth, you would think that moms would never have a second baby. But most couples go on to have more than one child. The pain is endured, as real and bad as it is, because what follows is incomparably good.

Think about a typical baby shower in which the increasingly uncomfortable mother-to-be sits at the head of the circle, soon to face even greater discomfort, and yet the games and celebrations begin. They don't call them labor parties, and they don't play contraction games. They are called baby showers, and everyone celebrates the joy that is to come when the pain is over. Keeping your perspective and focus on the joy to come will make all the difference when you are being carried deeper into a painful trial. It was said of Christ as he faced the pain of his crucifixion that he "for the joy that was set before him endured the cross, despising the shame"

(Hebrews 12:2). Christ fixed his mind on the happiness that he would experience on the other side of the unjust murder and suffering that he was about to bear. This mind-set, we are told, enabled him to endure his cross and despise the shame he was about to experience.

Thanksgiving

Our daughter, whom we were initially told was not expected to be born alive, was delivered by C-section very much alive, but in dire need of surgery. We met Stephanie face-to-face for the first time on a balmy Southern California evening two days before Thanksgiving. Her head was enlarged and her spinal cord was protruding out of her lower back. There was no time for bonding with our newborn. Two neurosurgeons were standing by to perform a delicate spinal closure and a critical assessment of her swollen brain.

Once Carlynn was rolled into recovery after the C-section, we were left to pray and wait for news concerning our daughter. As the hours passed we imagined every conceivable prognosis. We had to keep reminding ourselves of the good promises of God. We were assured that none of this was a surprise to him, and prayed that in tangible ways, God's grace would prove to be sufficient for each of us. As the clock approached midnight, the quiet of the dimly lit hospital room was interrupted by the voice of our daughter's lead surgeon. He began with the "bad news, good news" report.

The bad news was that Stephanie was paralyzed from the knees down and would have digestive and urinary challenges for the rest of her life. The good news was that her spinal closure went well, and with another surgery to her limbs and the proper leg braces, he expected that she would one day walk. In regard to her brain, the surgeons were not certain. They wanted to put off brain surgery, hoping that the swelling might resolve itself. We'd have to wait and see. We'd know within days, the surgeon told us.

We spent Stephanie's first Thanksgiving in the neonatal intensive care unit. The cafeteria turkey didn't compare to Carlynn's, but we had much to be thankful for on that memorable Thursday. Stephanie was recovering, and though paralysis and future surgeries were on the horizon, we knew the "bad" of all that we were trying to cope with could not be compared to the good that God had planned for his children. Our prayers for our daughter, our neighbors, our friends, and ourselves always came back to what was most important—the realities that will matter a thousand years from now. We knew then, and still know now, that limbs and organs that don't work as intended—as well as pain, suffering, and tears—are temporary. For now we are called to endure and to keep our minds set on the things above.

Keep Singing

Painful, dark days and nights met with thanksgiving are incomprehensible realities to both non-Christians and shortsighted Christians. But they are more common among God's people than we may think. Throughout the pages of the Bible we see God's suffering saints enduring their hardships while singing songs of praise and thanksgiving. Unjustly incarcerated, chained up in stocks, and badly beaten, Paul and Silas at "about midnight" were "praying and singing hymns to God" (Acts 16:25). They sang not because they enjoyed the pain or relished the injustice but because, as Paul wrote from a different jail cell, "for to me to live is Christ, and to die is gain" (Philippians 1:21).

This heavenly minded perspective makes all the difference. One day our suffering will be replaced by joy and permanent happiness. And while we have no right or license to expedite a premature departure from this life, we know that as difficult and as long as life's trials may be for us, we have an incomparably good future that will overshadow all of life's troubles. So let's thank God today for where we're heading, and tell him we'll purpose to joyfully endure any painful circumstance with a song of praise. With this life and eternity distinctly in perspective, let us join our voice with Habakkuk's and sing:

> Though the fig tree should not blossom, nor fruit be on the vines, the produce of the olive fail and the fields yield no food, the flock be cut off from the fold and there be no herd in the stalls, yet I will rejoice in the LORD; I will take joy in the God of my salvation. GOD, the Lord, is my strength; he makes my feet like the deer's; he makes me tread on my high places (Habakkuk 3:17-19).

CHAPTER 6

The Patience that Comes from Hope

George Matheson was born in Glasgow, Scotland, in 1842. He knew a lot about pain and suffering, for he was blind. And along with the variety of challenges and inconveniences that come to a man who is blind, Matheson's suffering was compounded by a number of painful events. He lost his sight, along with his chosen career and a number of friends, during his college years. And most painful of all, he lost his fiancée, who told him she could not imagine going through life with a blind husband. Years later, on the day his sister—who was his most loyal and loving caregiver—left home to marry, George sat down and dictated a poem that would eventually become one of the favorite hope-filled hymns of the church.

> O Love that will not let me go,
> I rest my weary soul in thee;
> I give thee back the life I owe,
> That in thine ocean depths its flow
> May richer, fuller be.
>
> O Light that followest all my way,
> I yield my flickering torch to thee;
> My heart restores its borrowed ray,

That in thy sunshine's blaze its day
May brighter, fairer be.

O Joy that seekest me through pain,
I cannot close my heart to thee;
I trace the rainbow through the rain,
And feel the promise is not vain,
That morn shall tearless be.

O Cross that liftest up my head,
I dare not ask to fly from thee;
I lay in dust life's glory dead,
And from the ground there blossoms red
Life that shall endless be.[1]

George Matheson understood that in the midst of pain help is found not by pulling away from God, but by drawing near to him. He knew that during times of suffering our faith needs to be deepened and our perspective must be lengthened in order for us to find the peace and perseverance that is required to live as we ought—especially when the pain doesn't seem to go away. He knew the importance of patience.

God called George into pastoral ministry, and Scotland's blind preacher would often stress the importance of patience to his congregation. He regularly exhorted his congregants that when life hurts they must learn to be confident in the hope of that "brighter" and "fairer" day that God has planned for his children. He would tell them not to wallow in their grief or sorrow, but to learn to be patient and carry on day by day with a godly anticipation of that "tearless" morn. Here are his words from one memorable sermon:

> To lie down in time of grief, to be quiet under the stroke of adversity, implies a great faith; but nothing requires greater strength than to work. To have a heavy weight in our hearts and still to run the race; to have anguish in our spirits and still perform our daily tasks. The hardest

thing is that most of us are called to exercise our patience, not in the sickbed, but in the busy street of activity.[2]

Patience doesn't come easily, but when it comes to suffering it is essential. If we haven't learned to wait well, then we haven't learned one of the fundamental virtues of the Christian life. We know that "in the world [we] will have tribulation" (John 16:33), often a kind that lingers for months and even years. So we must learn to patiently endure while confidently waiting on God's promised deliverance.

The Perils of Impatience

In our have-to-have-it-now, downloadable, microwave generation we would all admit that we hate to wait. No matter how trivial the wait might be. Whether it's at the airport security checkpoint, in five o'clock traffic, or in a slow drive-through line at the fast food restaurant. When we know what we want and getting it becomes a slow process, we quickly grow impatient. Add pain to the delay, and the wait can be almost unbearable.

> The Bible is big on patience because impatience will do us a lot of harm.

Right now you might find yourself in the middle of an agonizing wait for physical relief, emotional comfort, relational reconciliation, or financial rebound. Whatever it may be, when the days turn into weeks, and the weeks turn into months, it is easy to begin to lose heart and grow bitter. Giving in to that kind of emotional fatigue and the temptation to become an impatient person is understandable, but hang in there. God wants you to learn patience and he wants your heart to be fortified with strength and endurance.

The Bible is big on patience because impatience will do us a lot of harm, much more than just leading us to be discouraged. God warns us that impatience is the cause of a hundred lesser evils. Let's consider just a few of the negative and destructive consequences of impatience, and let's think of this list as a set of symptoms that should alert us that we are in need of a fresh perspective on the problems we face.

1. Complaining

Unfortunately today complaining is so common, even among Christians, that few seem to realize it is sinful. The Bible sees it as such a problem that it is prohibited entirely (Philippians 2:14). It is such an offense to God that we are told our complaining words and attitudes provoke his anger. During the Israelites' desert wanderings in the Old Testament—which was an understandably trying situation—the Bible states, "The people complained in the hearing of the LORD about their misfortunes, and when the LORD heard it, his anger was kindled" (Numbers 11:1).

If you know something about the timeline of events during the desert wanderings, it is important to note that this response from God came *before* the twelve spies were sent into Canaan. It came *before* the people resolved to disobey God, and the Israelites were sentenced to wander for forty years. The episode of complaining that provoked God's anger came with the expectation of entering the Promised Land. During this time God was faithfully supplying food, water, guidance, and leadership. Sure it was tough and uncomfortable, but the Promised Land was on the horizon.

Tragically, the Israelites' impatience regarding the difficult travels and what they considered to be second-rate food fueled an attitude of moaning and complaining that ignited God's anger and stern discipline. In the New Testament, Paul warns us not to follow their example by letting our difficult circumstances feed the kind of impatient grumbling that can provoke God's stern correction (1 Corinthians 10:10-11).

When my wife and I were experiencing the emotional pain and difficulty of our daughter's surgeries and the less-than-hopeful prognoses, the following challenge was often made clear in our minds:

We must handle this situation without the immature grumbling and complaining that would be shamefully recalled when God eventually brought us through to the "brighter" day and "tearless" morn. We knew it would arrive. If not in this life, certainly in the next. The last thing we would want is to look back on the months or even years of moaning and griping about how terrible it was. The promised land for Christians is always on the horizon. Though temporal relief may be months away, and eternal relief may be many years away, we must resolve not to allow our impatience to lead us to complain.

If you find that the pain in your life has led to an increase in complaining, confess it, see your need for patience, and ask for God's gracious endowment of perspective, hope, and self-control.

2. Outbursts of Anger

Almost without exception, the impatient person becomes an angry person. Impatient people become mad at life, and often become mad at God. This anger then spills over onto everyone around them. And of course their outbursts of anger do great damage in almost every area of life. Proverbs 29:22 tells us that "a man of wrath stirs up strife, and one given to anger causes much transgression." When we get impatient and frustrated, we imagine that our anger is appropriate and maybe even constructive, but the Bible is clear that such outbursts don't result in anything good or righteous (James 1:20).

We are helped in our suffering by the closeness of friends and family, but anger does nothing but drive them away. Intuitively, our friends will do as the Bible instructs—they will pull back from us when we are given to outbursts of anger (Proverbs 22:24-25). When we are suffering, few things are more self-injurious than to allow our impatience to turn us into angry and irritable people.

Thankfully, if we realize that in our present trial we have been given to emotional tantrums, God is gracious to forgive. Let's confess our anger and seek his merciful cleansing. Then let's resolve to repair our relationships. Of course we need to deal with the impatience that fuels our anger—which we will seek to do in this chapter—but we should not delay in reaching out to reconcile with those whom we have repelled. It is amazing how God's grace can abound in our relationships when we humbly accept responsibility for our angry outbursts and seek the forgiveness of others.

3. Idolatry

Idolatry may seem like a long way from impatience, but it really isn't. Consider how quickly the Israelites fell into worshipping the golden calf because they were impatient when Moses delayed in coming down from Mount Sinai (Exodus 32:1-2). The people felt a void of leadership and a rising urgency regarding direction, protection, and solutions. God's prophet was late in returning, and the Israelites decided to look elsewhere for hope. Stating it like that may begin to give us a better picture of what idolatry actually is. We don't have to bow down to a pagan image to be idolaters. Simply put, idolatry takes place in our hearts when we begin to move our trust, confidence, and hope from God and his revealed truth to something else. It can be anything else. During painful trials we can easily make idols out of our doctors, our lawyers, our bank accounts, or even our own thoughts and plans.

Obviously God is in favor of us having doctors, lawyers, and bank accounts. He is also in favor of us thinking rational thoughts and making good plans. The question is, What are we trusting in? In the Old Testament we read of a righteous king named Asa who served God faithfully for many years. But near the end of his life, when he encountered two serious trials, one political and one medical, his trust began to shift. On the political front, as a battle was brewing on his northern border, King Asa, moved by fear and impatience, decided to break with his former pattern of trusting the Lord and sought to build an unorthodox alliance with a powerful foreign king. He bribed this king to attack his enemy on their opposing border. Rather than seeking the Lord and trusting him for a success-ful defeat of his enemy, Asa put his trust in a foreign king and in a shrewd but unsavory political move. God points out his impatient idolatry and tells him of the victory and the prosperity he had for-feited by his lack of faith.

On the medical front, the aging Asa had contracted a serious dis-ease in his feet. But instead of putting his confidence in God, the Bible says, "Even in his disease he did not seek the Lord, but sought help from physicians" (2 Chronicles 16:12). The impatient King Asa quickly called the doctors, putting his idolatrous trust squarely in their education, insight, and expertise, with no thought to the One who could have, and likely would have, spared his life. Sadly, this subtle form of idolatry cost him his life.

Just as the faith-filled King David utilized chariots and horses in battle, so we will utilize doctors, medications, and surgeries. But as David sang, "Some trust in chariots and some in horses, but we trust in the name of the Lord our God" (Psalm 20:7). As David's son Solomon taught, "The horse is made ready for the day of battle, but the victory belongs to the Lord" (Proverbs 21:31). No matter what our painful trials might be, let us always keep our trust planted in our sovereign and all-powerful God.

4. Apostasy

Of greater concern than complaining, anger, and even idolatry is the prospect that painful trials can lead to apostasy. The last thing God wants to see in the midst of our trials is that we turn our backs on him. We should always guard our hearts, but there is no time more critical for us to stand guard over our thoughts, emotions, and motives than when we are hurting.

The Bible shows us that apostasy often springs from impatience when "the going gets tough." Think about Judas, who surely on the surface looked as committed to Christ as any of the other disciples. But the Bible tells us that his motives were twisted. When it became

clear that the kingdom of Christ on earth was not going to be inau-
gurated anytime soon, and that following Christ involved a cross
not only for Jesus but some kind of painful suffering for all of his
disciples, Judas decided he wasn't up for the wait. In his impatience,
Judas decided to cash in his investment for whatever he could get
out of it now.

Judas's defection wasn't unique. The Bible says there will be many
in every generation who sign up for the blessings and benefits of
Christianity, but will choose to bail out when they realize those
benefits aren't immediate and that they are not immune from suffering. Jesus said that many will receive the word of the good news
of Christ, but will only endure "for a while" because "when tribulation or persecution arises on account of the word," they will "immediately" fall away (Matthew 13:20-21). Their hope of the good that
ultimately comes from following Christ will be overshadowed by
their impatience.

Make sure your faith in God is genuine, the kind that is in this
for the long haul, regardless of how long you may have to wait for
the blessings and pleasures of his coming kingdom. Be certain you
understand that Christianity will always involve waiting, and therefore it will always require that you develop the supremely important
virtue of biblical patience.

Patience and Hope

In the last chapter we spent some time looking at the ultimate
hope of the future good that God has planned for us. A key point
was the fact that the extreme good of that coming reality is far more
intense than the intensity of the bad that any of us could ever experience here on this fallen planet. Now we need to see how a proper
focus on the future good God has planned for us can and should
develop our ability to patiently wait without complaining, getting angry, or exhibiting any of the other destructive expressions of

impatience. Notice the relationship between Christian hope and biblical patience in this key text of Scripture:

> We ourselves, who have the firstfruits of the Spirit, groan inwardly as we wait eagerly for adoption as sons, the redemption of our bodies. For in this hope we were saved. Now hope that is seen is not hope. For who hopes for what he sees? But if we hope for what we do not see, we wait for it with patience (Romans 8:23-25).

This extremely important passage speaks of the patience we so badly need, and is filled with practical insights that can help us acquire it. Let's spend the rest of our time in this chapter on patience looking at each element contained in this passage. Let's start at the bottom and work our way up. First let's consider the obvious—hope-fueled patience means that we wait and don't give up.

Wait for It—No Quitting

At some point in a book about suffering the following needs to be said: God wants us to patiently wait for the relief he has promised. No quitting. No checking out. No thoughts of ending it all.

So far I've used words like *excruciating, agonizing,* and *almost unbearable.* I know the pain of suffering personally. I have had a front-row seat to knowing many who have suffered more intensely than I have. And I have read broadly of the extreme suffering of other Christians throughout church history and around the world today. Even as a child, when I learned about the men and women of the Bible, I came to appreciate something of the depth of pain experienced by many of God's choice servants. As a pastor I have watched many come through the darkest seasons of their trials with a patient endurance and a strengthened character. But I'm sad to say that I have also seen others decide to end it all. I have been called to their homes and then had to officiate the funerals of several who have taken their own lives.

While those who have never suffered to any great degree may roll their eyes and say, "How could anyone even think of taking their own life?" those who have experienced great and abiding pain know the temptation. This is true even for those who were closely connected to God. Job felt it after the death of his children (Job 3:11-22). Elijah felt it when he was put on the most-wanted list (1 Kings 19:4). Moses felt it when the people continually turned against his leadership (Numbers 11:15). Jonah felt it when God wasn't doing what he expected God to do (Jonah 4:3). Paul felt it while on the run from his enemies (2 Corinthians 1:8). And when we add to this temptation that as Christians we have an amazing promise of ultimate relief, profound joy, and unending happiness on the other side of this life—it is easy to see how ending it all may be an enticing thought.

While imprisoned in Rome Paul described this Christian "death wish" when he wrote,

> For to me to live is Christ, and to die is gain. If I am to live in the flesh, that means fruitful labor for me. Yet which I shall choose I cannot tell. I am hard pressed between the two. My desire is to depart and be with Christ, for that is far better. But to remain in the flesh is more necessary on your account. Convinced of this, I know that I will remain and continue with you all, for your progress and joy in the faith (Philippians 1:21-25).

Even the apostle Paul admitted that he desired to die because that was "far better," but he refused to pray that way, let alone take any steps to make that a reality. He knew that life was something that God gave, and something that only God should choose to take away. The timing is up to God, not us. Our job is to do whatever good it is that God has called us to do for as long as God gives us life. It is morally wrong to murder someone else, and it is also morally wrong to murder ourselves.

In the Bible, many godly people have felt the temptation to "stop waiting" for God's promised relief. But it is those who opted to end it all who are portrayed as committing an ungodly act. Men like Judas and King Saul are not hailed as those who relied on God, but as those who chose to forsake him.

If this is a serious temptation, or even just a recurring thought for you amid your suffering, I strongly encourage you to keep reading and take hold of the patience that God makes available to you by his Spirit. And don't struggle through this alone. Get other strong Christians involved in bearing your burdens. Call your church, get in contact with your pastor, and talk to your family and friends. Seek the help you need to endure through this trial. Realize that giving up is not God's will for your life, and that he can do much with your life for his glory as you choose to trust him and tenaciously endure through the pain.

The "Unseen Hope"

We read in Romans 8 that biblical patience is built on a hope that is unseen.[3] That doesn't mean it is an irrational or illogical hope. As a matter of fact, nothing is more rational than to bank on the promises of a God who has always kept his promises throughout hundreds of years of recorded biblical history. And nothing is more logical than to trust in the promises of a Christ who physically rose from the dead, appearing to hundreds to assure them—and us—of the good things he has in store for those who trust him. Nor does "unseen" mean that this hope is something ethereal or ghostly. As we have already noted in the last chapter, our promised future is tangible, real, physical, and concrete. We will live in a material kingdom, in biological bodies, engaging in genuine activities, and having real experiences.

> The high point of God's promises to us are not yet fully realized.

What is meant by the idea of unseen hope is this: The high point of God's promises to us are not yet fully realized. Yes, a lot of good

things happen when we become a Christian—our sins are completely forgiven, we are legally made children of God, and we receive
the gift of God's indwelling Spirit, just to name few. But recall our
passage in Romans 8, where Paul wrote to a group of Roman Christians that "we wait eagerly for adoption as sons, the redemption of
our bodies. For in this hope we were saved" (verses 23-24). The
emphasis is on the future. The focus is on a final and ultimate phase
of our adoption process. Earlier in the same passage we are told
this completion will come at the time when "creation itself will be
set free from its bondage to corruption and obtain the freedom of
the glory of the children of God" (verse 21). That time when God
"makes all things new" and when his plan of salvation and renewal
"is done" certainly isn't now (Revelation 21:5-6).

The problem for many suffering Christians is the following
assumption: They believe that because they are God's children, have
God's Spirit, and are the object of God's favor that things should be
going a lot better for them than they are. But the point of Romans
8 is that the current phase of the Christian life is one of hope—a
future hope. We haven't arrived. We are not there yet. The Christian
life is primarily about something we've yet to experience. Remember
Paul's words: "Now hope that is seen is not hope. For who hopes for
what he sees?" (verse 24). In other words, if we assume that the fulfillment of the promises of the Christian life are already here, then
there would be no future hope for Christians—we'd be experiencing it all now. But of course we are not, nor should we expect to. The
goal is to remember that while we have various blessings now, the
main point of the Christian life is still in the future. When we suffer
and fail to understand this basic arrangement, discouragement and
disillusionment are all but guaranteed.

Remember the summer road trip from your childhood? It was
likely peppered with the oft-repeated phrase, "Are we there yet?"
Yes, school is out for the summer, we are on vacation, and we are on
our way. But no, we are not at the final destination. No, we are not

there yet. How cruel it is for modern preachers to tell their congregations that they've arrived when in fact they haven't. To that point Paul wrote, "If in Christ we have hope in this life only, we are of all people most to be pitied" (1 Corinthians 15:19). The journey may not be easy. The air conditioner may go out, we may get carsick, and it may take a lot longer to get there than we thought. We may even have several scuffles with our brothers and sisters along the way. But just wait—where we are going will make it all worthwhile. This is the focus of biblical Christianity, and it is one that should motivate us to hang in there and wait patiently. Yes, even wait eagerly for the arrival of the ultimate kingdom!

The Role of the Holy Spirit

Our passage in Romans on biblical patience began with the reminder that Christians don't wait alone. We have the Holy Spirit residing in us. And that makes all the difference when it comes to being able to wait well. God's incredible gift of the indwelling Holy Spirit in our lives is described in Romans 8 as the "firstfruits" (verse 23). That is a way of referring to the giving of the Holy Spirit as "the first of God's gifts"[4] or "as the first part of God's promise."[5] While we have yet to arrive at the place where we will receive all of God's blessings, one of the most important blessings we have already received is the gift of God's Spirit.

To fully appreciate this we need to take a minute to consider who the Holy Spirit is. As complex as this may be, God has told us that he has eternally existed as one God in three Persons—the Father, the Son, and the Holy Spirit. So while each Person of the Godhead may have different roles, each Person of the Godhead is fully God. So when we speak of the indwelling Holy Spirit, we are saying that God *himself* relates to us in a very personal and direct way. God lives in us and relates to our spirit, working in us to prompt us, convict us, and direct us.

In the familiar verses about the work of the Holy Spirit in our lives, we are told "the fruit of the Spirit is love, joy, peace, [and] patience" (Galatians 5:22). And that makes perfect sense. If God dwells in us, we should see evidence of God's presence and interaction in our spirit. He is a God of love, a God of joy, a God of peace, and he is certainly a God of patience. Actually, there is no one more patient than God. More people test his patience every day than anyone else has ever or will ever be tested. The Bible describes his patience as "perfect patience" (1 Timothy 1:16).

Consider how long he waits. You and I have been on the planet for only a handful of decades. We have never had to wait for anything even for a fraction of the time that God has been waiting for a variety of things. Peter has us consider how long God will wait to inaugurate Christ's kingdom just so more people can be brought into it. Peter wrote, "The Lord is not slow to fulfill his promise as some count slowness, but is patient toward you, not wishing that any should perish, but that all should reach repentance" (2 Peter 3:9). Now we know that from the time the Holy Spirit had Peter write those words, close to 2000 years have passed. That is a powerful ability to stay the course and wait.

That same God dwells in us. He is committed to working in us as we cooperate with him. He will motivate, inspire, train, and prompt us to wait well. He is the expert when it comes to waiting with endurance. One of the more antiquated ways older English Bibles used to translate the Hebrew and Greek words in the Bible that we now translate "patience" was "longsuffering."[6] That may not be a word we use much anymore, but it captures well the goal for us as Christians. We need to aspire to see God's Spirit produce in us the ability to "suffer for a long time" without breaking down, giving up, or bursting out in anger.

There may be a lot of things our wise heavenly Father refuses to give us when we ask, but the effects of the Holy Spirit is not one of them. God is so generous to step up the work of the Holy Spirit in our lives when we humbly and sincerely ask.

You may feel like you are not good at waiting. You may consider yourself an impatient person. God's indwelling Spirit is ready, willing, and able to change that. The powerful Spirit of God is the internal resource of every genuinely converted child of God. Reach out to God in prayer even now. Ask for more of his prompting, conviction, training, and guidance as moment by moment you seek to patiently wait, and even eagerly wait, for the relief God has promised.

CHAPTER 7

Learning to Pray Through the Pain

I once read in the news of a woman who gave birth to her baby while driving. I'm sure you've heard stories of moms who have given birth in the passenger seat or the backseat of a car. But this story was different—this mom actually gave birth behind the wheel.

While driving down US Highway 2 in Minnesota, this pregnant woman went into labor, had her water break, and started having her baby. Later, when asked by reporters what she did at that point, she said she put the car on cruise control, scooted the seat back, and had the baby. Amazing! She was traveling down the highway at 70 miles per hour and she didn't even pull the car over. While she was giving birth, her husband, who was sitting in the passenger seat the whole time, reached over and took control of the steering wheel.[1]

When I recall this incredible story, I am reminded of the Christians I know who are in great pain but who just keep plowing through life. They desperately need to stop to ask for help and to attend to the crisis in their life, but they stubbornly refuse to do so.

As I have already noted, great pain in our lives should be understood, in one sense, as God shouting to get our attention. Whatever the cause for our crisis of pain, it should prompt us to slow down, pull over, turn to God, and seek him in prayer.

Let the Pain Prompt More Prayer

When my older brother and I were kids, we would periodically "go to war" against each other using our little toy army men. We would "pick teams" and sort through the green plastic warriors, which were outfitted with sniper rifles, grenade launchers, and bayonets. I would always skip the guy with the phone in his hand and the pack with the long antenna on his back—in my childhood assessment, he didn't appear to be helpful. Every time I passed on this guy, my war-savvy brother would remind me how stupid I was. He'd say, "That's your communications guy—when your soldiers are attacked, wounded, or surrounded you'd better have one of those guys or you won't be able to call headquarters and get the help you need."

That was good advice. And it still is. When we are attacked, wounded, or surrounded in the Christian life, few things are as important as communicating with "headquarters." When times get tough we dare not neglect our critical link to our Maker. How tragic it is to see Christians who are under attack and hurting, but are not running to God in prayer. Christ knows our pain, and as one personally and physically acquainted with the sufferings of human life, he stands ready to help us in our time of need. As one hymn writer put it over 150 years ago:

> What a Friend we have in Jesus,
> All our sins and griefs to bear
> What a privilege to carry
> Ev'rything to God in prayer!
> O what peace we often forfeit,
> O what needless pain we bear,
> All because we do not carry
> Ev'rything to God in prayer![2]

The sentiment of these lyrics goes back much further than 150 years. The hurting and suffering people of God have been singing songs about the importance of praying through their pain for more than 3000 years. In Psalm 34, when David ran for his life while King Saul's army sought to hunt him down, David reminded his genera-tion that God's ear was attentive to the cry of his people when they suffered and that "the Lord is near to the brokenhearted" (verse 18).

Earlier we addressed the fact that God doesn't always deliver us from our trials the moment we cry out to him because he has good plans to accomplish in our difficult times. But we should note that God has promised to always stay near to his children when they call out to him—especially when they are hurting. When we are suffer-ing, we have a unique opportunity to cultivate a kind of intimacy and closeness with God that few other circumstances allow.

The Closeness of God's Spirit

When we cry out to God in the midst of our trials and seasons of pain, the Bible tells us that God's Spirit is actively involved in our praying. Romans 8 states it this way:

> Likewise the Spirit helps us in our weakness. For we do not know what to pray for as we ought, but the Spirit himself intercedes for us with groanings too deep for words. And he who searches hearts knows what is the mind of the Spirit, because the Spirit intercedes for the saints according to the will of God (verses 26-27).

This is an amazing and even surprising passage. But before we look at what it says about how we should pray when we are hurt-ing, let's quickly address three curious topics that frequently surface when we ponder this text.

1. What Is Meant by Groanings?

Jumping into Romans 8:26-27 without reading and under-standing the surrounding context can give rise to all kinds of bizarre misconceptions about what is meant by the statement "the Spirit himself intercedes for us with groanings too deep for words."

It is essential to note the pattern of the *groaning* theme that Paul has been using throughout this passage. Just prior to saying that the Spirit is "groaning" in his intercession (verse 26), the text tells us "the whole creation has been groaning" (verse 22) and that during our painful trials we Christians "groan inwardly" (verse 23).

Groaning is a word that depicts the expression of frustration, pain, sadness, and desire for relief, which is felt when we are in painful trials. Elsewhere in the New Testament, the Greek word used here is translated "to sigh." In the Old Testament book of Ezekiel, the few in Jerusalem who were "sighing and groaning" over the sinful decline of the city of Jerusalem were praised and blessed by God because of their sadness over the things that were not the way they ought to have been (Ezekiel 9:4).

Romans 8 poetically speaks of creation as though it were a person. It is said to be groaning because of its "bondage to corruption" (verse 21). Remember that in Genesis chapter 3 the physical world was cursed by God and subjected to all kinds of problems because of the rebellion of Adam and Eve. Romans 8 informs us that creation is groaning in anticipation with an "eager longing for the revealing of the sons of God" (verse 19). The idea here is that the fallen and broken physical world can't wait for this long period of sin and suffering to end.

Romans 8 then goes on to say that suffering Christians are also groaning as they "wait eagerly for adoption as sons, the redemption of our bodies" (Romans 8:23). We too sigh with a frustration and sadness about the way things are today. While living in fallen and broken bodies in a fallen and broken world, we too groan with anticipation for this period of sin and suffering to be over.

It is against this backdrop that Paul writes in verse 26 that the Spirit of God who lives in us is active in our prayers as an intercessor. He sighs and grieves with sadness over the present state of things in this fallen world. He is longing, along with us, for that new day when sin, suffering, and pain are no longer a part of our experience. In other words, the Holy Spirit deeply empathizes with our plight and feels for us in our suffering. He aches, as do we, for the day when this will all be in the past. He will help us in our praying—not as an unfeeling prayer partner, but as one who groans with us in this broken world as we cry out to God in our prayers.

2. Who Is Our Intercessor?

For some, this idea of the Spirit *interceding* for us may seem confusing. "Isn't Jesus our intercessor?" some have asked. The answer is "Yes!" as this very passage goes on to tell us: "Who shall bring any charge against God's elect? It is God who justifies. Who is to condemn? Christ Jesus is the one who died—more than that, who was raised—who is at the right hand of God, who indeed is interceding for us" (Romans 8:33-34).

Clearly both Christ *and* the Holy Spirit are our intercessors, but in two different ways. Christ intercedes—that is, he intervenes or mediates—on our behalf by providing for us a perfect human life in the place of our imperfect and sinful human lives. He also intercedes for us by having provided a complete payment for human sins by suffering in our place on the cross. In this sense Jesus Christ stands and intervenes on our behalf so that we are accepted rather than condemned by the Father for our sins.

The Holy Spirit, on the other hand, is described as interceding or intervening for us in our praying. He is compassionately adjusting, changing, and even substituting his requests to God for the ones we offer (more on that in a minute).

> We have two divine intercessors—one in heaven and one on earth.

Another important distinction between Christ's intercession and the Spirit's is the location in which that intercession takes place. A point that is repeatedly made in the Bible is that Christ is physically present at the right hand of God (Psalm 110:1; Romans 8:34; Hebrews 1:3). Of course, Jesus is fully aware and sympathetic to everything in our lives—so much so that he is sometimes said to be with us or in us (Matthew 28:20; Colossians 1:27). But it is Christ's departure back to the Father that initiated the sending of the Holy Spirit to dwell personally in us and with us (John 16:6-7). Jesus told his disciples that he was leaving, and that the Spirit would be sent to live in his followers and be with them every day of their lives.

So then, we have two divine intercessors—one in heaven and one on earth. Jesus intervenes for us in heaven before the Father as the One who makes it possible for God to consider us holy and acceptable. The Holy Spirit intervenes for us as our indwelling prayer partner, making our prayers appropriate and acceptable to God.

3. What's So Weak About Our Prayers?

Romans 8:26-27 gives us a humbling reminder that there is something weak and inadequate about our prayers. Earlier we talked about our natural tendency during tough times to simply ask God to take the pain away. There is nothing wrong with praying that kind of prayer—at least for a while. But, as we learned, that is not always God's will. He plans to use our seasons of pain to bring glory to himself, to make us more obedient, to confirm to us the reality of our faith, and to bring us along in spiritual maturity—just to name a few reasons. In the words of Romans 8:28, "all things work together for good, for those who are called according to his purpose."

Of course the Holy Spirit fully understands all the details of the good purpose that the Father has planned to accomplish. And he also knows how each trial is going to serve that purpose. Obviously, the Holy Spirit is fully informed. And it should be just as obvious that we are not. Our praying is seriously handicapped because of our limited knowledge, not to mention the way that pain always prompts a kind of praying that cries out for the pain to end immediately. We need the Spirit's intercession because when it comes to our prayers during suffering, "we do not know what to pray for as we ought" (verse 26).

Your Blind Spots in Prayer

It is easy to admit that the Holy Spirit knows better than we do about our needs when we find ourselves in painful situations. But maybe our prayers will never get to the humble and flexible place they need to be until we explore a little more thoroughly just how limited our knowledge actually is when we bow our heads to pray. Let's take a couple of minutes to consider a few of the blind spots we can easily have when we pray.

1. We Can't Always See God's Will

I distinctly remember taking our firstborn son to the doctor for his first vaccinations. I recall the empathy I had for my unsuspecting child, who I knew was about to erupt into tears. Worse was the look he gave me when he started crying—a look that communicated, "Dad! What is going on? Why are you letting this happen?" Ugh. Not only was I "letting it happen," I had scheduled it and was paying for it to happen. He, of course, couldn't understand that these painful shots were for his own good, and were precisely what I had planned for him.

One of the reasons our prayer requests are sometimes wrong is because we can't always clearly perceive the will of God. Think back to the situation when the apostle Paul prayed for his thorn in the flesh to be taken away (2 Corinthians 12:7-10). Whatever the painful ailment was, Paul prayed that God would simply take it away and heal him. We are safe to assume that Paul, like us, wanted to pray prayers that were consistent with God's will. But the truth was that this chronic illness was God's will for Paul. That may seem cruel, but God's good plan for Paul was that this ailment would be used to keep him humble and dependent on Christ in light of his incredible privileges and fame as a prophet and apostle.

Paul's prayer changed as he came to realize that for the remainder of his life, God was going to use this ailment for good. But thankfully, according to Romans 8, we can be sure that the Holy Spirit was praying the right prayers from the very beginning, because the Spirit knew God's will for Paul and the good purposes the Father had planned. If it was possible for the apostle Paul to initially pray in a way that was at odds with the will of God, certainly it is possible for us to do the same.

Unfortunately, having pain in our lives tends to drive our focus toward short-term prayer concerns, whereas the will of God almost always aims at the longer-term development and progress of our lives. Jesus regularly sought to get us to think about the big picture, while calling us to see that the immediate circumstances—as contrary as they may appear—are sovereignly designed to take us there. Consider his illustration of the vine and the branches in John 15. Jesus stated that he is the vine, we are the branches, and the Father is the vinedresser. He said that every branch that bears fruit, because it is abiding in him, the Father will prune so that "it may bear more fruit" (verse 2).

It would seem that if we are abiding in Christ and bearing fruit, all would be good. Why not leave the branches alone? But the truth of this teaching from Jesus is that growing, fruit-producing Christians will be pruned so that they will bear even more fruit. Though Christ doesn't give us any details concerning the pruning process, it certainly speaks to something painful.

So if your current pain happens to be part of God's pruning process, it is understandable that you would be praying for it to go away. But as Jesus taught, this painful season is designed as part of God's perfect will for your life. It is not God's discipline to bring you to repent over some sinful decision. It is not the painful reaping from some foolish choices. It is not suffering that is associated with being a part of a fallen world. In this case, if it is the pruning of God, it is the loving and perfect will of God, and it will be used to make you a more productive Christian.

2. We Can't Always See the Spiritual Battles

When Christians in the armed forces are deployed to war zones, their prayers, along with the prayers of their loved ones, become very focused and specific. When soldiers are in a conventional war they know it and intuitively begin to pray for their safety in light of the anticipated threats and hazards of the battlefield. In a similar manner, we are in the midst of a variety of spiritual battles that are waging right now, which we cannot see or perceive. And because we are unaware of much of what goes on in the spiritual realm, our prayers can end up being way off base.

For example, there was a day when Jesus turned to Simon Peter and said,

> "Simon, Simon, behold, Satan demanded to have you, that he might sift you like wheat, but I have prayed for you that your faith may not fail. And when you have turned again, strengthen your brothers." Peter said to him, "Lord, I am ready to go with you both to prison and to death." Jesus said, "I tell you, Peter, the rooster will not crow this day, until you deny three times that you know me" (Luke 22:31-34).

What do you think Peter prayed about that morning? Maybe he prayed about the preparations for the upcoming Passover celebration. Maybe he prayed about the need for people to respond rightly to the teachings of Jesus. Maybe he had some concerns about the relationships among the disciples and prayed for God to unify the team. Who knows? But obviously, based on Peter's response to Jesus, he hadn't prayed about the major assault that Satan was planning to launch against his faith and loyalty to Christ.

Jesus could see this battle forming, but Peter could not. Peter was praying about who knows what, while Jesus was praying for Peter's faith not to fail. Much like the current role of the Holy Spirit in our lives, Jesus was praying for the urgent and important things on Peter's behalf, while Peter was busy praying for other less important things—all because Jesus could see the upcoming spiritual battles and Peter could not.

This had to be a lot like the day when Satan approached God concerning Job. Imagine what Job might have prayed about that day. I'm certain it wasn't about the battle that would soon come upon him. He couldn't have known about the scene that took place in the spiritual realm as described in the first chapter of Job. His ignorance would continue for some time, even after thieves began to steal his possessions, storms killed his children, and diseases broke out on his skin. His prayers, even in the midst of his pain, were uninformed—because he could not see the spiritual conflict that he was embroiled in.

The Bible says, "We do not wrestle against flesh and blood, but against the rulers, against the authorities, against the cosmic powers over this present darkness, against the spiritual forces of evil in heavenly places" (Ephesians 6:12). The awareness that there's a lot we are *not* aware of when things happen in our lives should motivate us to pray differently. We cannot confidently toss out *obvious* and *logical* requests about our situation when there may be a lot more going on that we couldn't possibly know. We need to pray with a deference to the Holy Spirit's concerns, as the passage goes on to say (Ephesians 6:18). He knows exactly what is happening, why things have happened the way they have, and what specifically should be done next. We, on the other hand, have a limited perspective.

3. We Can't See the Future

It should go without saying that one of our obvious blind spots is the future, and that should affect the way we pray. Sure there are some basic things about the end times that God's Word has revealed, but as to what will happen to you or me tomorrow, we just don't know. Knowing this information is one of the exclusive characteristics of God. The details of our future are uniquely known to him alone.

The Bible chides Christians for a kind of arrogant praying that approaches God as though we know what tomorrow will bring. We dare not be presumptuous in our praying.

James wrote:

> Come now, you who say, "Today or tomorrow we will go into such and such a town and spend a year there and trade and make a profit"—yet you do not know what tomorrow will bring. What is your life? For you are a mist that appears for a little time and then vanishes. Instead you ought to say, "If the Lord wills, we will live and do this or that." As it is, you boast in your arrogance. All such boasting is evil (James 4:13-16).

While this passage doesn't specifically address our praying when we are suffering, it can certainly apply. How often do we assess our painful situations, assume the future trajectory of our lives, and pray accordingly? We offer up prayers that presume—if God would do this or that, then everything would work out just right down the road. We imagine that tomorrow would be just as it ought to be—if God would just prevent this or that. But in fact, we really don't know what other factors God may have ordained to be a part of our tomorrows.

A quick assessment of our past prayer requests should convince us of this point. How many times have we prayed that God would do something specific to change a painful situation, but as he unfolded our future, we could see that had he answered our presumptuous prayers the way we asked, it would have been all wrong? In such cases we can thank God that he did not answer our prayers as we had laid them out. Because we couldn't see the other aspects of our future which God had planned, our prayers were weak and inadequate. The good news is that the Holy Spirit knows every factor concerning our future. We can trust that his prayers for us are the right ones.

Admitting that we can't see the future, anticipate spiritual battles, or in many cases know God's will for our lives lets us learn to pray differently. First, and most obviously, let us learn to pray with a godly flexibility.

Flexible Praying

Flexible praying is the kind of praying that James has already prescribed for us: "If the Lord wills" (verse 15). From our limited vantage point, there must always be an "if" attached. Yes, in the midst of our tough times we should lay out our requests to God, but we must be sure to show our humble deference to the wisdom of God—"If that is want you want." Even Jesus prayed in this way when he spoke to the Father about the prospect of bearing our sins on the cross. He said, "Let this cup pass from me; nevertheless, not as I will, but as you will" (Matthew 26:39).

That is an important scene to remember, especially when we're tempted to think that this kind of praying is feeble or pathetic. It's not. It's godly, wise, and biblical. It is how Jesus taught us to pray when he included the phrase "your will be done" in the model prayer of Matthew 6:9-15. It is certainly the kind of praying he practiced in his own life. And it is the kind of praying we see from godly men and women throughout the Bible.

Consider one of the most painful episodes in King David's life—when his son Absalom launched a temporarily successful coup against his reign in Jerusalem. As David was forced to leave the royal palace because of the uprising, the priests came to ask him what to do with the valuable and sacred furnishings of the temple. David told Zadok the priest to leave them in the temple in hopes that this would be a short-lived trial, and that he would be back to worship on the Temple Mount. Though David admitted that perhaps he wouldn't be back, he certainly wanted this unjust and unwarranted revolution to be quelled. However, he said of God, "Here I am, let him do to me what seems good to him" (2 Samuel 15:26).

Just after that, as David and his entourage were evacuating the capital city, one of his detractors, a man named Shimei, came out to curse and throw rocks at the fleeing king. David's commander asked if he could have permission to go over and kill this malicious opportunist. David said, no— "If he is cursing because the Lord has said to him, 'Curse David,' who then shall say, 'Why have you done so?'" (2 Samuel 16:10).

On the surface this may seem pathetic. But David understood that God had a plan in this terrible season of his life. And if all that was happening to him was ultimately wrong, then God would vindicate, restore, and reverse the situation. Of course that is what David and his loyal cabinet members desired and prayed for. But they were willing to accept this major defeat in their lives—if it was what the Lord willed. As you probably know, this painful situation was only a temporary detour for King David and his men. God did vindicate his anointed king, and Absalom and Shimei paid dearly for their spiteful rebellion.

> Always remember to keep an open mind about what God might be doing in your situation.

When things are seemingly out of control in your life, pray. Lay out your requests clearly, but don't hold on to them too tightly. Always remember to keep an open mind about what God might be doing in your situation.

Confident Praying

It may seem like an oxymoron, but the best praying is done with a kind of confident flexibility. Our prayers must be flexible because we all have to admit that we have blind spots. But our praying should also be confident because we don't pray alone—we have a divine prayer partner who intercedes for us every time we bow our heads to talk to the Father.

Picture it as a scramble round of golf with the world's best golfer. In a scramble format you and a fellow golfer play as a team instead of competing as individuals. You both tee off and hit your best shot. If his shot is better than yours (which, because he's the world's best golfer, it always will be), you will both proceed to the spot where his shot landed, and you will both take the next shot from there. So even if your drive fell short, or if you shanked it out of bounds, you get the advantage of moving to where the expert placed his shot. That's how a scramble round of golf is played—you both take the shot, but you only have to play the best shot.

With those rules, some terrible golfers are saying, "I'd play more golf if it worked like that." Well, when it comes to our praying, it does work like that. When we pray, the Holy Spirit prays with us and for us. God then responds, and the next time we pray, the Holy Spirit again intercedes for us with the better praying. And God again responds, and we move forward.

At this point you might be asking, "If that's how it works, then why pray at all?" Good question. The answer is simple: Those are the rules! Just as in a scramble round of golf, I am not allowed to stay in the clubhouse and have lunch while I send the world's best golfer out to the course. Scramble golf is a team sport. Those are the rules. I am required to step up to the tee box and take a shot, and then my partner takes his shot. Likewise, God has called us to pray—especially when we are hurting. He wants to hear from us. He wants us to slow down, pull over, and talk to him about what's happening in our lives. We can be confident that as Christians, we will never pray alone. The loving, all-knowing, all-powerful Spirit of God will pray with us through the pain.

Confident Flexibility

When, on the first day of her life, our newborn daughter Stephanie came out of spinal surgery, the surgeons said that all things considered, she had done well. However, as they admitted her to the neonatal intensive care unit, their nagging concern was that the swelling in her brain seemed to be continuing. They thought she might need a second surgery for the insertion of a permanent drainage valve.

Anytime a parent hears the words *potential surgery*, the prayer request seems obvious. Add to that the word *permanent* in reference to what they wanted to implant in Stephanie's brain, and we knew what we wanted God to do for her. After Stephanie's spinal surgery the doctors had said that there was a possibility that the ventricles in her brain might begin to drain on their own. So we, along with our friends and family, prayed fervently, laying out our very clear and specific requests. "Please God," we asked, "there are so many risks and complications associated with this type surgery and this kind of equipment. Please just let those ventricles drain, and let our little daughter avoid another major surgery."

Of course, the biblical thing to add to this and every other prayer is, "If it's your will, Lord." God knew what he had planned for our infant daughter, and we could confidently rest in the fact that our Father cared for her and that the Holy Spirit was interceding on our behalf. And so we prayed as we continued to measure the circumference of her head every few hours. As disappointing as it was to us at that time, her head did in fact continue to swell, until finally a red line had been crossed and the surgeons prepared for the second surgery. While we were praying for our daughter to avoid brain surgery, God's Spirit was obviously interceding differently with requests— for the particular surgeons, the new brand of medical equipment, a perfect fit, a successful implantation, and a number of other things that had never crossed our minds.

Obviously, this second surgery was something we would have chosen to skip, but God had a plan. Much of it was yet to be understood at that point, but we were confident as far as our faith would allow. We were trusting as best we could that God was doing something which, in the long run, would glorify him. Even during the complications, we had to admit that God was in this, and that we could trust him.

Trusting God was important for us, and it is just as important for you. Every follower of Christ can boldly trust in the sovereign oversight of God, knowing that regardless of how bleak and chaotic life may seem, the Lord has a good plan. You can confidently trust that God is at work in the midst of your trials. What he wants from you now is to keep praying through your difficult days with a confident flexibility. While you can't possibly see the whole big picture quite yet, you can rest in the truth that God loves you, and that his Holy Spirit stands ready to pray with you through the pain.

CHAPTER 8

Looking for the Good
When Things Go Bad

The old caricature of the dismissive doctor telling his patient, "Take two aspirin and call me in the morning" can begin to sound a lot like the words we hear from our well-meaning friends or church leaders when we are hurting. Of course they want to help, but often their words sound shallow and less than comforting.

The book of Job shows us how frustrating it can be to be on the receiving end of trite platitudes and misguided counsel when we suffer. For much of the book, Job's three friends pile on their hollow words, at one point leading Job to blurt out, "Miserable comforters are you all. Shall windy words have an end?" (Job 16:2-3).

When those around us, in their attempts to be supportive, toss out phrases that seem canned and too simplistic to be helpful, we may begin to lose heart. Considering the complexity of our struggle or the depth of our pain, their seemingly naïve perspectives can sound to us like a string of superficial clichés.

One of the phrases we are almost certain to encounter during trials is the well-worn line, "Well remember, God works all things together for good!" That sentiment may not sit well with us, especially when we try to associate the word *good* with a death in the family, a debilitating illness, or a devastating financial collapse. And yet before we roll our eyes and conclude that this line is an overused cliché, we should take note that these words are lifted directly from the Scriptures. And that the context for those divinely inspired words is one in which the apostle Paul is addressing Christians who were undergoing serious trials and suffering.

Hollow Words or an Amazing Truth?

One of the reasons we receive as hollow the words intended to comfort us is because we assume that the person delivering them knows little of the pain we are experiencing, or has never encountered any profound pain himself. However, when it comes to the promise, "We know that for those who love God all things work together for good, for those who are called according to his purpose" (Romans 8:28), this is the wrong assumption. Let's take a minute to ponder the two sources of this incredible claim.

First, consider the human source—the apostle Paul. If you know anything about the life and ministry of Paul, you know things were not cushy for him. He certainly knew what it was to suffer. Read slowly through this summary list of his experiences, which are found in Paul's second letter to the Corinthians (11:23-27). Imagine the pain and all the associated loss involved in each of these situations:

- imprisonments
- countless beatings
- often near death
- five times received forty lashes less one
- three times was beaten with rods
- once was stoned
- three times was shipwrecked

- a night and a day was adrift at sea
- on frequent journeys
- in danger from rivers
- in danger from robbers
- in danger from his own people
- in danger from Gentiles
- in danger in the city
- in danger in the wilderness
- in danger at sea
- in danger from false brothers
- in toil and hardship
- through many a sleepless night
- in hunger and thirst, often without food
- in cold and exposure

That is quite a list. Paul did not live insulated from pain. If anyone could know that God can work good out of pain, it would be Paul. Were he sitting with you right now, and you explained to him your current struggles, he would certainly identify and probably recount some similar situations from his own life that brought about equally great pain or hurt.

Paul knew what it was like to see God work his painful circumstances together for good. And while I'm sure that the complete picture of the good in every painful situation could not be fully understood this side of heaven, Paul would later look back on his life and write these words: "The Lord stood by me and strengthened me, so that through me the message might be fully proclaimed" (2 Timothy 4:17). Paul's calling and purpose in life was "fully" fulfilled! His task was completed. And though he bore many scars and memories from his suffering, he would go on and confidently insist that "the

Lord will rescue me from every evil deed and bring me safely into his heavenly kingdom" (verse 18).

Think of that. We know Paul was the target of many evil plots. We know that he suffered from chronic physical ailments. And from the history that followed this letter we know that the Romans executed Paul for his missionary efforts. Yet his testimony is that the goal of his life was fully completed and that there was no real or lasting damage because he knew he'd be safely brought into God's heavenly kingdom.

So when Paul wrote to the Christians in Rome who were facing their own set of struggles and trials, he knew what he was talking about. His words of promise in Romans 8:28 were not wishful thinking or shallow platitudes intended to gloss over their pain and provide a nice-sounding fantasy to get them through their dark days. Paul himself could testify that the suffering we face in this life is not purposeless or random. He had seen God's good hand in his own life—working out a plan that, in the end, would result in something eternally positive.

That's Paul's background and perspective, but we must never forget that the God-breathed words of Scripture always have a second and ultimate Author (2 Timothy 3:16; 2 Peter 1:21; 3:15-16). These words come from God himself. So the promise "We know that for those who love God all things work together for good" are not just Paul's expectation, they are more importantly God's own promise. And the promise is not only to the first-century Roman Christians, but also to all "those who are called according to his purpose" (Romans 8:28). That includes you.

> God doesn't make promises he can't keep, and there is never anything hollow about his assurances.

In case our reading of the Old Testament might cause us to imagine that God was largely insulated from the experience of pain and suffering, the New Testament should resoundingly destroy that myth. Not only did God the Father experience the pain of giving his Son as the sacrifice for our sins, but God the Son personally suffered the atrocities of a Roman crucifixion, which was an excruciatingly painful method of execution. Add to this that God the Holy Spirit has personally and intimately walked every suffering child of God through the crushing pain of every trial that he or she has ever faced, and we can be certain that the One who offers this simple and straightforward promise knows what it is to suffer. There is nothing unfeeling, detached, or unsympathetic about his saying that "all things work together for good."

We should also remember that the triune God who makes this promise is the One who has the power to ensure its fulfillment. He is not *wishing it* for us. Being the Author of Romans 8:28, he guarantees that when we suffer it will actually result in something that will accurately be considered *good*. God doesn't make promises he can't keep, and there is never anything hollow about his assurances.

Making Sure the Promise Applies to You

Recently on television I saw a home video of a cruel prank that a husband pulled on his wife. He had given her a fake lottery ticket, which declared that they were the big winners of a huge jackpot—but of course they weren't. As expected, she jumped around in excitement, joyfully shouting at the thought of their unbelievable good fortune. Slowly the euphoria subsided as she double—and triple-checked her ticket and then noticed the small print that made it clear she had won nothing. Her elation quickly turned into embarrassed frustration and a series of punches to her amused husband's shoulder.

While this prank resulted in a hearty laugh from a TV audience, you have to feel for this woman. She was temporarily convinced that she had won some great benefit that she, in fact, had not. It's bad enough to be elated for a few minutes about the illusion of wealth you'll never enjoy, but to spend months or years expecting your trials to be worked together for good and to never have it actually happen is far worse. And because God's promise in Romans 8:28 is a conditional promise, this may actually be the tragic experience for some who try to claim it. Let's make sure that's not you!

God's amazing promise in Romans 8:28 goes like this: "We know that for those who love God all things work together for good." The verse is very clear that this guarantee is made to *"those who love God."* If you don't "love God," then this is not a promise that you can or should claim as applying to you. And so we need to make certain that we really understand what it means to "love God."

1. Do You Love the Real God?

On the surface, the condition in Romans 8:28 seems pretty broad. Some might ask, "Don't most people love God?" Actually no. At least not the *real* God—the God of the Bible. Many people who cheerfully claim to love God are actually in love with a god of their own imagination. This is the tendency of many who want a god yet also want to live by their own standards. They think that the God of the Bible is too restrictive, and they would rather love a variation of God, a god whom they've tailored to fit their own preferences and practices.

This is nothing new. Notice how this Old Testament psalm of Asaph describes a lot of people today—people who say they love God but in reality have forgotten him altogether.

> You give your mouth free rein for evil, and your tongue frames deceit. You sit and speak against your brother; you slander your own mother's son. These things you have done, and I have been silent; you thought that I was one like yourself. But now I rebuke you and lay the charge before you. "Mark this, then, you who forget God, lest I tear you apart, and there be none to deliver!" (Psalm 50:19-22).

The wide variety of ideas and opinions about God come about in part due to God's grace—in that he is holding back his immediate judgment of sin. His temporary *silence* when people disregard his commands allows people to assume that God must be "one like them," agreeing and approving of their own values and practices. Of course God has revealed the truth about who he is and what he approves, and to love God is to love the only God there is—the one we read about in the pages of his Word.

So if we want to rest and rejoice in the promise of some real *good* coming from our suffering and pain, the real question is this: Do we love God—the *real* God, or are we devoted to a god we have fashioned after our own liking?

2. Do You Have Real Love for God?

Maybe you are already well acquainted with the God of the Bible. Perhaps you've spent plenty of time in a good Bible-teaching church and have a pretty clear and accurate view of God based on what is written in Scripture. Still, a problem may exist that prevents you from qualifying for the promise of Romans 8:28. Do you love God with a *real* biblical love?

Biblical love for God is more than an affection for or a set of good feelings about God. It includes a kind of devotion or allegiance to him that is evident in our daily lives. Having a *real* love for God makes a radical and obvious difference in the way we live. The Bible says, "This is love, that we walk according to his commandments" (2 John 6). Earlier the apostle John wrote:

> By this we know that we have come to know him, if we keep his commandments. Whoever says "I know him" but does not keep his commandments is a liar, and the truth is not in him, but whoever keeps his word, in him truly the love of God is perfected. By this we may know that we are in him: whoever says he abides in him ought to walk in the same way in which he walked (1 John 2:3-6).

Really loving God results in a profound shift that moves people from living "for themselves" to living "for him who for their sake died and was raised" (2 Corinthians 5:15). No matter how sordid or how culturally acceptable your life may have been before you became a follower of Christ, this kind of profound internal reorientation always produces a kind of life-change that is summed up in the familiar words of 2 Corinthians 5:17: "If anyone is in Christ, he is a new creation. The old has passed away; behold, the new has come."

It should go without saying that Christians are not sinless (James 3:2; 1 John 1:8-10), but it is hard to overstate the fact that a Christian's *real* love for God will result in a desire to sin less and take seriously the call to obey God each and every day.

So before we rush to claim the promise that "all things work together for good" in the midst of our pain and suffering, let us be sure we are actually among "those who love God" (Romans 8:28).

Looking for the Wrong Kind of "Good"

If you are among those who have *real* love for the *real* God, then you can be confident that "God works all things"—even the worst of your struggles and pains—"together for good." But when you go looking for the *good* he is working out, be sure you are not just looking for one type of good—the short-term, temporal kind of good.

There are those who suggest that if you love God and your house burns down, the *good* that God is going to work out is giving you a bigger and better home. Or perhaps if you are a Christian single and your girlfriend dumps you, the *good* God is going to bring about will be to grant you a friendlier and more attractive girl. Or they say that if you get fired from a great job, of course the *good* will be a better, higher paying job.

> We tend to think in terms of tangible good, when perhaps God wants to give us spiritual good.

Now there are times that these things happen. And I suppose there are some who could testify to them actually happening in their lives. But the promise in Romans 8:28 has a much bigger and longer-term *good* in view. And the good won't always be in the same category of life. Consider again Paul's thorn in the flesh, which he wrote about in 2 Corinthians 12. Paul was afflicted with a physical ailment that, as far as we can tell from his New Testament epistles, was never cured or healed. He did not have this ailment, as some would suggest today, so that these symptoms would drive Paul to the doctor in order that a more serious disease might be discovered and could be remedied before it was too late. No, Paul's physical sickness, which would never go away, was used to promote an aspect of his *spiritual* health—namely, his humility, which was essential for his productivity in preaching and proclaiming the gospel.

So when we find ourselves in financial trials, a health crisis, or a relational collapse, we should not wrongly assume that such things are only a precursor for soaring finances, better health, or perfect relationships. Sometimes our losses are permanent, yet they are used by God to create, bolster, safeguard, or expand some other good that he is working in our lives. We tend to think in terms of tangible good, when perhaps God wants to give us spiritual good. And that brings us to another interesting and important phrase that is attached to this promise, which may help us get a better sense of the good that God is planning to work from our current trial.

Advancing God's Good Purpose in Me

Take note of the last phrase in Romans 8:28: "We know that for those who love God, all things work together for good, *for those called according to his purpose.*" This amazing promise of God puts the focus on the fact that those who love him are those who have been "called according to his purpose." One of the obvious problems with looking for the short-term and personal *good* in our suffering is that the promise speaks to *his* purpose and not ours. While his purpose obviously includes us, the *good* he desires to do won't necessarily have to do with our personal preferences for a bigger house, a better job, or an improved relationship. His purpose is bigger and better.

The immediate context of Romans 8:28 reveals one very important aspect of this purpose—one that relates to our personal lives. The next verse says, "Those whom he foreknew he also predestined to be conformed to the image of his Son" (Romans 8:29). To put it simply, God plans on making us less like our old selves, and more and more like Christ. The patterns of our behaviors, our values, the words we use, the thoughts in our minds—all of these are included in "his purpose" to continually transform us into people who are more *Christlike*.

With that in mind, you can more easily see the breadth of the possibilities as God "works all things together for good" in your trial. If your house burns down, it is not hard to imagine that the good may not be a bigger house after all. Perhaps your relationship with your home and its contents is actually a barrier that is keeping you from being more like Christ. Maybe the downsizing that results is the freeing step that launches your life into a new level of Christlikeness and godliness. The same may be true with an irreparable disability from a car accident, a chronic illness, or a broken relationship. The good you should be looking for might be found in the answer to the question, "How does this painful trial refine my character to be more like Christ?"—which is precisely what God has purposed for your life.

If you spend enough time with Christians who have suffered profoundly, you will hear story after story of how their pain, suffering, and trials have changed them to reflect more consistently the heart, values, and patterns found in the life of Jesus Christ. How often I hear Christians say, "I wouldn't trade my disability [my loss or my disease] for anything in the world, in light of the way God has used it to change who I am to be more like Christ." That is the kind of incomparable good that so many people tend to overlook when a crisis strikes.

At this point it may be helpful to recall the kind of prayer that we discussed in chapter 3. Remember the things that we wanted our prayers to include? They were concerns like reordered priorities, increased and more consistent obedience, assurance that our faith was genuine, and an increasing depth of spiritual maturity. Christ is the ultimate model of all of these things, and they are the kinds of things that we ought to anticipate and eagerly look for in the wake of our pain and suffering.

Advancing God's Good Purpose in the World

God has called us for purposes that include good intended for more than just ourselves. Yes, God has purposed to bless us, but the emphasis of our instructions for the Christian life is focused on the way God has called us to be a blessing to others. Often our suffering is part of the preparation that the Lord has sovereignly chosen to take place in order to make that a reality.

When Jesus and the disciples encountered the blind man in John 9, the disciples asked Jesus, "Rabbi, who sinned, this man or his parents, that he was born blind?" (verse 2). This revealed the common assumption that people had—when people suffered, it was probably because God was punishing them in some way. But a person with congenital blindness posed a particular problem for the disciples' theory. Could the man have sinned prenatally, or was God imposing a punishment in advance for something the man was going to do as he grew up? Or was God using the man's blindness as a punishment against his parents for something they had done?

Jesus responded by pointing out, as we saw earlier in this book, that not all suffering is directly related to someone's sin. In this case, Christ told his disciples, the man's blindness was so that "the works of God might be displayed in him" (verse 3). Think of it—this blind man and his family endured years of sorrow and serious inconvenience so that Christ might demonstrate his credentials as the Creator. In addition, the man was born blind so that Christ might provide a powerful spiritual lesson to the Pharisees, as well as to the generations of people who would read of the account in John 9 for the next 2000-plus years. That man's suffering not only resulted in his coming to faith and the forgiveness of his own sins (verses 35-41), the purpose was much broader than that. This man's blindness was imposed on him by God—for our good, and for the good of millions of others.

Consider some of the specific ways God may use your trials and pains for good in the lives of others.

1. To Win Others to Christ

In the broadest terms, our purpose as Christians is to glorify God (1 Corinthians 10:31). When people become Christians and confess the lordship of Christ, God is glorified (Philippians 2:11). If in some way our painful trial brings someone to the place of repentance and new life in Christ, we would have to admit that our suffering has worked together for good—major good!

After our infant daughter came out of her second surgery—in which a shunt had been implanted in her brain and the doctors discussed the prospect of a third surgery to reconstruct Stephanie's deformed and paralyzed feet so that with the use of leg braces she might one day be able to walk—I sat down and put together a website. I wasn't sure how, but I figured that perhaps if people outside our church could hear her story, God might use it as a vehicle for sharing the gospel. And I thought perhaps I could show how Christian families deal with suffering like Stephanie's, and this might serve to point people to Christ.

It didn't take long to realize that Stephanie's suffering, as well as ours, was not only saving people spiritually, but physically. Before we heard any of the stories of repentance and faith, we heard several stories of physical lives being saved. Because spina bifida is one of the most commonly diagnosed prenatal deformities, it is also a major medical reason parents are encouraged to abort their children. Just as several doctors matter-of-factly urged us to terminate our daughter's life, many parents have received similar counsel from their doctors. Just by sharing our trials, victories, and setbacks, along with many pictures of our daughter, stories started to trickle in of parents granting the gift of life to their unborn children who had also been diagnosed with prenatal deformities.

It is amazing how the serious struggles and pains in life can open doors for discussing issues like abortion, repentance, and faith in Christ with non-Christians. It would be hard for us to know for certain how many lives have been saved, both physically and eternally, through the story of our daughter's battles with spina bifida. And if that were the *only* good that came from the congenital disease in Stephanie's life (and it's not), it would be enough to enthusiastically say—in the face of a seemingly devastating diagnosis—that God "works all things together for good."

How might God utilize your loss, pain, trial, or suffering as something that could be leveraged for the gospel? How would it change your perspective to think that someone or some group of people might become members of the family of God and eternal citizens of the kingdom of heaven because you are going through your trial? Look for that profound good in whatever the bad circumstance might be.

2. To Spur Others On in Doing Good

We are told in Hebrews 10:24 to "consider how to stir up one another to love and good works." The Greek word in this passage that is translated "consider" is a strong word that involves more than just casual thinking. We are told here to seriously ponder the way in which we can be utilized by God to spur on and motivate other Christians to love God, love people, and to do what is right.

When we suffer, we have opportunities that we wouldn't otherwise have. As we saw in Stephanie's crisis, people can be inspired, encouraged, motivated, and challenged to live more zealously for Christ just by watching the way we respond to our challenges. As we look to Christ and seek to glorify him in our trials, we'll find that fellow Christians who are walking through our pain with us are naturally stirred to find hope, endurance, and patience in their own circumstances.

This is not about putting on some phony appearance of godliness and a stoic pretense that tries to act like your pain doesn't hurt. It's about letting people into your life and letting them know your heart as you honestly seek to keep your focus on Christ. It's about looking for the good that is being worked out and exercising the faith that regardless of your circumstances, God is going to get you through them.

How often have you gone to a hospital or a graveside in hopes of providing comfort and encouragement, only to find that the person going through the painful situation—simply by their confident trust in God—ended up ministering to you instead? And spurred you on to love God more and live more faithfully for him? When you suffer, be that person. Not by being fake, but by nourishing your resolve to trust God in the midst of your pain.

3. To Prepare You for Ministry

We are all called to minister to our fellow Christians and "bear one another's burdens," "encourage the fainthearted," and "help the weak" (Galatians 6:2; 1 Thessalonians 5:14). We are most effectively taught how to do that—and how *not* to do that—when we are burdened, fainthearted, and weak. When we are suffering, we learn from experience what helps, what comforts, what encourages, and what doesn't. God has been working on us through his Word, his people, and his leaders to get us through our seasons of suffering. What we learn about encouraging and helping can become invaluable assets in our lives, which, in turn, can be used for God's glory in the lives of others.

The Bible goes so far as to say that some of the trials in our lives are given for this specific kind of training. Read these words carefully:

> Blessed be the God and Father of our Lord Jesus Christ, the Father of mercies and God of all comfort, who comforts us in all our affliction, so that we may be able to comfort those who are in any affliction, with the comfort with which we ourselves are comforted by God. For as we share abundantly in Christ's sufferings, so through Christ we share abundantly in comfort too. If we are afflicted, it is for your comfort and salvation; and if we are comforted, it is for your comfort, which you experience when you patiently endure the same sufferings that we suffer. Our hope for you is unshaken, for we know that as you share in our sufferings, you will also share in our comfort (2 Corinthians 1:3-7).

Your trials can be seen as the training ground in which God prepares you to be a blessing and a comfort to the people in your future who will be suffering. In time, your current season of pain can be drawn upon as a tremendous resource that will not only give you the ability to say, "I know how you feel" and "I know what you are going through," but as you are careful to maintain a strong relationship with Christ, you can actually provide the essential guidance to keep your fellow Christians from losing heart and shipwrecking their faith.

It is difficult to find a Christian who is being used effectively in counseling, teaching, training, or preaching who has not been prepared by God for that work through at least one or two seasons of extreme pain and suffering. Even if you haven't signed up to be used by God in those ways, your current pain may be something the Holy Spirit wants to use in your future for the good of other Christians. So take notes on how God comforts and heartens you. You may find those notes useful in your conversations with others in the months or years ahead.

4. As Cautionary Tale

Growing up as the younger brother, I am oddly grateful for the way my big brother's struggles, dilemmas, and problems were logged in my inquisitive little mind as road maps for sidestepping the avoidable landmines of youth. Of course I made several missteps that he didn't, but his experiences became helpful cautionary tales that spared me from similar hassles. While I won't wait around for the "You're welcome" from my big brother, I am thankful.

As we considered early on, some of the suffering and trials in our lives can be traced back to our own sins, failures, or imprudence. When that is the case, our season of pain can glorify God by becoming the reason other people avoid the same suffering in their lives. Consider the generation in the Old Testament who wandered in the desert for forty years because they had cowered at the spies' report and failed to trust God's promise that he would enable them to take the Promised Land. Centuries later, Paul told the Corinthian Christians to remember their failure and pain—to learn from it, and to not do what the Israelites did (1 Corinthians 10:1-13). "Now these things," he wrote, "took place as examples for us, that we might not desire evil as they did" (verse 6). That one generation's painful season of desert wanderings has arguably been the reason that countless numbers of Christians have chosen to trust God and do the right thing when they faced their own tests of faith.

Even our daughter's spina bifida, though not traceable to a sinful decision, has certainly motivated us to persuasively speak to numerous parents about the importance of women supplementing their diet with folic acid—which, when deficient at conception, has been shown to contribute to these kinds of neural tube spinal defects. It is encouraging to think that in our sphere of influence, God has been glorified through Stephanie's disability by promoting better prenatal health and possibly a few less congenital defects.

5. God Knows What Else

When considering the good that God will work in and through the "all things" we suffer, it is difficult not to think of Joseph's words in Genesis 50. He had been rejected by his brothers, thrown in a pit, continually lied about, sold as a slave, framed, and wrongly imprisoned. But years later, after being reconciled to his brothers, he confidently testified, "You meant evil against me, but God meant it for good" (verse 20).

In Joseph's situation, God was working a big plan to relocate him to Egypt. Eventually God would have Joseph work his way from prisoner to the royal court so that he might be the wise advisor who managed the country during a historic famine. This, in turn, saved not only millions of Egyptians, but also Joseph's own family from Israel. While you and I may not be a part of God's international plan to rescue a nation, we should learn from this Old Testament example. We never know what good God might be working in the lives of others through the pains we are made to endure. As in Joseph's case, it might take several years for us to begin to catch a glimpse of what God is doing. But don't give up. Keep looking.

A Promise Is a Promise

The promise we have been considering in Romans 8:28 is a divine promise. The God who cannot lie has said, "We know that for those who love God all things work together for good, for those who are called according to his purpose" (Romans 8:28). Those are true words for God's children. And they can be profoundly comforting.

While I can't point to a passage in the Bible that guarantees we will see and understand the good in a matter of months or even years,

I am confident in our trustworthy God—that he is working out a good plan. If we don't see it clearly in this life, let's keep looking. For on the other side, we will see every last struggle and painful circumstance as a sovereign and wise part of God's perfect plan. Take heart and keep looking. You will see it—either in this life or in eternity.

CHAPTER 9

Faith in the Goodness of God

All of this talk about God using the bad things we experience for good purposes can be comforting and reassuring. But often just the fact that we, our family members, friends, and people around the world experience so much suffering and pain can rattle our faith in the goodness of God. And because of all the evil we will continue to deal with and see in our world, it is important and helpful for us to think through and shore up our understanding of the goodness of God despite the reality of evil.

The Problem of Evil

When I converse with a non-Christian about the claims of Christ, almost always he or she brings up the perennial question: "Why would God allow all the suffering and evil that takes place in this world?" That's a great question, one that comes into sharp focus when we study the nature and attributes of God as presented to us in the Bible.

In Scripture, God has revealed himself to be all-knowing, all-powerful, and completely good. So when babies are born with debilitating deformities, for instance, the Bible asserts that God certainly knows about it, that it is something God certainly has the power to prevent, and that it seems to be in obvious contradiction to his goodness.

This leads skeptics to state, "Perhaps God *isn't* aware of what's happening down here, or he is too weak to stop it, or maybe he isn't all that good after all." Or, as some atheists and agnostics would suggest, perhaps there is no God at all.

It is one thing to say that God uses all the bad things in his people's lives for good, but it is also important for us to grapple with the question of how God can be all-knowing, all-powerful, and all good and allow any of *the bad* in the first place.

The Reality of Evil

It may sound bizarre, and it may even be hard to believe, but some philosophers, world religions, and cultists through the centuries have attempted to answer this question by insisting that there is actually no such thing as evil in the universe. "It is all an illusion," they say. But trying to pretend that disease, destitution, and death really don't exist provides little help for those suffering with their effects. Being told by gurus to separate ourselves from the grief or pain because it is not real convinces few and adds a whole new set of problems for those trying to understand God and their lives.

If the Bible is God's definitive word on reality, then we should be quick to dismiss such empty proposals. We need to know that the Scriptures repeatedly underscore the fact that there are many people and things that can accurately be called *evil*. Just a quick skim through the Bible will present us with all varieties of evil beings, evil behaviors, and truly painful realities. All of these people, actions, and experiences are treated as serious problems that can't be wished away or ignored.

I should also be careful to make the point that just because Christians can and should confidently insist that "for those who love God all things work together for good" (Romans 8:28), this should never take away from the fact that the bad things we encounter are truly bad. Knowing that God will work my daughter's disabilities, surgeries, and daily struggles into something truly good should never cause me to say that spina bifida, hydrocephalus, and paralysis are good things. They are not. They are bad—really bad! Our family may accept their presence in our daily lives as part of God's sovereign plan to work out something good, but nowhere does the Bible suggest that we should see disease, sickness, or disability as good things.

This misunderstanding of sickness, disease, and death is often spoken of in eulogies and sermons at funerals. How often have we listened to well-meaning people say that we need to embrace death as a "part of life," or some variation thereof, which attempts to assure us that death is somehow a good thing? Yes, we can agree that for the Christian there is something good on the other side of death. And we can rejoice that God has a sovereign plan in the timing of every birth and every death. But to pretend that death itself is a good thing is to miss the clear statements of the Bible regarding death itself. Death was the wretched sentence imposed on sinful mankind (Romans 6:23). It is called our enemy (1 Corinthians 15:26). Even with the prospect of an immediate resurrection, standing before the dead body of Lazarus prompted Christ to shed tears over death's reality (John 11:35).

Understanding Evil

When thinking through the problem of evil many will pose the question in this way: "Why did God create evil?" That may be a common way to ask the question, but it's not a great way to think about the problem. Before we try to answer where evil came from, it would be good to recognize that evil is not a thing that can be created. It's not a thing at all. It is a *description* of things. It rightly describes people, actions, attitudes, and a lot of other bad realities.

When the idea of evil is introduced in the Bible, the scene is later described in terms of sin, transgression, and iniquity. To put it in the words of the Bible, "All have sinned and fall short of the glory of God" (Romans 3:23). Evil is a description of things—in this case, human decisions that don't measure up to the holy, perfect, and right standards of God. Evil is a way to describe things not being what they ought to be.

Maybe the analogy in 1 John 1 can prove helpful in driving this important definition into our minds. John wrote, "God is light, and in him is no darkness at all" (verse 5). Just as we would affirm that darkness is a reality, what we are describing by *darkness* is really the absence of light. God is good, all good. There is nothing but good in God. Unfortunately, as 1 John goes on to emphasize, the problem is that there is a lot which *does not measure up* in the world—a lot of things that can be rightly described as *darkness*. There is a significant *absence* of the good that God is—both in our world and in our lives.

When we talk about the reality and presence of evil, we are actually describing the absence of the good, holy, and perfect things that God is and does. And the reason for this absence of good is bound up in the unique creatures that God made "in his own image" (Genesis 1:26-27).

The Story of Moral Agents

The Bible sets the stage for describing the entrance of sinful actions, and all their painful consequences on the planet, by explaining the uniqueness of the beings who chose to fall short of God's perfection. Unlike the material universe and the diversity of animals on the earth, the Bible tells us that men and women were created with an exclusive dignity and grandeur. They were created in God's image and reflected his own capacity to be rational, emotional, and volitional. Their powerful ability to think abstractly, creatively, and imaginatively was combined with the complex experience of participating in all the sensitive feelings, passions, and sentiments that we can all attest to. Beyond that, man and woman were endowed with the power of making deliberate, voluntary, and conscious choices that had far-reaching effects.

The account describing God's creation of the first man and woman repeatedly stresses that these powerful and complex beings were created good. They were crafted without flaws. These thinking, feeling, deciding persons were without any inherent defects or shortcomings. God created people who were just as they should be. They had a wide variety of capacities as beings made in God's image, but they were created without anything falling short of God's glory and perfection.

Their *fall* into sin, which is laid out in Genesis 3, describes how these volitional beings made their own choices—permitted by God to stand as their own. God did not force submission to his perfect standards. He allowed them the dignity of making decisions that were their own—even if they were wrong. Looking back on how it all turned out may lead us to see this power of choice as a risky or hazardous gift. But as we learn later in the Bible, even in their failure to comply, God had a well-thought-out plan that would bring glory to himself and show great mercy to fallen people.

There is another important aspect of their sinful decisions to consider. It can be seen as the reason we are all able to sit around and ponder the problem of evil. When Adam and Eve exercised their power of volition in choosing to fall short of God's perfect standards, God graciously chose to delay the ultimate consequences of their decisions. Think about that for a minute. Had God immediately dealt with their sinful choices by carrying out the full, just, and equitable consequences for their decisions, earth would have been eradicated of all evil. They would have been eternally banned not only from their garden home, but also from earth, the presence of God, and from all of God's gracious gifts.

But God didn't do that. Yes, he imposed a number of just consequences on them (and us) for their sins, but he did not eradicate the earth of evil. Instead, God began to hint of his redemptive plan that could remove all the guilt and all the consequences of the sinful choices they had made. God decided to allow sinful people to inhabit his planet and to continue to make choices with their powerful decision-making capacities. He would not allow it forever, but he would allow it for a time—quite a long time, from our perspective.

It was because of the gracious choice of God to postpone ultimate judgment that we now live on a planet that is filled with a lot of darkness. Without this divinely given grace period every sinful decision would incur an immediate, eternal, and permanent solution, which would necessitate the removal of every sinner from God's planet and his blessings.

God's Just Sentence on the Planet

Speaking of the planet, in Genesis 3 we read about another decision of God that left the physical world in a lot of pain. God wisely chose to impose an appropriate sentence on the *ground*—which included the materials of which people were made. God's *curse* of the physical fabric of the universe would result in physical illness, disease, and death in our bodies, as well as all the problems we witness in our physical world.

We call this kind of evil *natural evil*. The existence of natural evil may best be understood as the Father's decision to not allow his rebellious children to harness a perfect, powerful, and sinless world for their own purposes. Sinful people would now be forced to live in a sinful environment that is subject to all sorts of natural rebellion. This unpleasant frustration of the physical world is a just penalty for mankind's sin, as well as a practical deterrent.

How encouraging it is to know that the physical corruption that God imposed on this world will one day be removed!

It is helpful to remember that just as God promised that moral evil would be temporary, he has also promised that natural evil would one day be reversed. Notice how every kind of suffering, pain, and evil will come to an end with the coming of Christ.

> For I consider that the sufferings of this present time are not worth comparing with the glory that is to be revealed to us. For the creation waits with eager longing for the revealing of the sons of God. For the creation was subjected to futility, not willingly, but because of him who subjected it, in hope that the creation itself will be set free from its bondage to corruption and obtain the freedom of the glory of the children of God. For we know that the whole creation has been groaning together in the pains of childbirth until now. And not only the creation, but we ourselves, who have the firstfruits of the Spirit, groan inwardly as we wait eagerly for adoption as sons, the redemption of our bodies. For in this hope we were saved. Now hope that is seen is not hope. For who hopes for what he sees? (Romans 8:18-24).

How encouraging it is to know that the physical corruption that God imposed on this world will one day be removed! This is an important truth to remember when you are encountering some painful aspect of this fallen, corrupted world. How often Carlynn and I have sat with Stephanie and found joy in the anticipation that one day there will be no need for surgeries, medications, leg braces, shunts, catheters, crutches, or wheelchairs. Every biological imperfection will be reversed and every "bondage to corruption" will be replaced with the "freedom of the glory of the children of God."

God's Good Redemptive Plan

In Christian circles we frequently hear the words *redeemed* and *redemption*. But those words fail to communicate the power and promise that they should when we don't fully appreciate the problem that they remedy. The word *redemption* is used repeatedly to describe and illustrate the work of God to *release* and *deliver* fallen creatures from the consequences of their sins.

The word was used of God's act of deliverance in Moses and Joshua's day. God released his people from the bondage of enslavement in Egypt to the joy of the Promised Land. As important and real as their oppression and emancipation were, they were only pictures of the reality that has eternal consequences for all of us. The Bible speaks much of sin's enslaving power (John 8:34; Romans 6:6; Titus 3:3). It is a kind of bondage that comes with a heavy price both here and now (2 Peter 1:4) and in the next life (Revelation 20:11-15). The good news of the Bible is that Christ came to earth and put on human flesh in order to live the life we should have lived, and to absorb the divine punishment on the cross that we deserve (2 Corinthians 5:21; 1 Peter 3:18).

Because this transaction solves the sin problem for those who have repented of their sins and put their trust in Christ, all the consequences of sin can and will be reversed. The payment for sins has been made and the effects of sin are promised to be withdrawn. As I have repeatedly emphasized in past chapters, those effects aren't all removed quite yet. We may now be relationally reconciled to God because of Christ, but we are still subject to many of the reverberating results of moral and natural evil. And we will continue to endure these until the time that God has ordained for "the revealing of the sons of God" and "the redemption of our bodies" (Romans 8:19, 23).

The Bible says that the whole plan to redeem fallen people and a fallen planet has been masterfully drawn up by God and will lead to the eternal celebration of his mercy and grace (Ephesians 1:4-14). We should not worry that anything was or is out of God's control, but instead we should be assured that this Master Planner "works all things according to the counsel of his will" (verse 11) and has included each of us, guaranteeing our perfect inheritance, "to the praise of his glory" (verse 14).

Whether it's the painful trials we face or the broad effects of sin we see around the world, we must affirm God's good management of all things and know that our sovereign God is working a masterful plan both on the smaller scale of our lives, and on the larger scale of human history. In the end we will confirm—with the rest of humanity—the perfect justice and inscrutable mercy of our Creator.

It is so important to make sure that we are participants in that mercy. We can joyfully anticipate the redemption of every ache, pain, crisis, and trial when we stand confidently by faith as a child of God. Knowing we have a right relationship with our Creator makes all the difference in the world. His redemption both spiritually and physically is for those who trust him for their forgiveness and acceptance. Be sure that is a reality in your life today. Place your trust in the finished work of Christ—knowing that it is his life and death alone that make you acceptable before God.

Avoiding Unbiblical Conclusions

In the attempt to figure out how God's sovereign oversight of all things coexists with the presence of evil in the world, some people have arrived at wrong conclusions and yielded themselves to foolish patterns of living. It has been rightly said, "If we are not careful we can begin to use biblical truths in unbiblical ways." When it comes to understanding God's sovereignty and the existence of evil, we must be very careful.

1. Sinners Are Always Responsible

When we consider that the fall of mankind ultimately put into action God's gracious plan of redemption, and that the suffering in our lives caused by people's sinful choices works together for good, then it is not a huge leap to begin to excuse sinners as those who are *helping God's plan along*. While some may argue that such a conclusion adds up theologically, in reality, it stands in serious conflict with several Bible passages. Sinners are always held responsible for their sinful actions. Sinning is *always* wrong regardless of the way God plans to use it for his glory and our good.

Consider the example of Christ's betrayal. This was clearly a part of God's plan, and needed to take place in order to initiate the trial and subsequent crucifixion of Christ, which resulted in our salvation and forgiveness. But the crafty, conspiring, and greedy treachery of Judas was clearly wrong and punishable. Jesus said, "The Son of Man goes as it is written of him, but woe to that man by whom the Son of Man is betrayed! It would have been better for that man if he had not been born" (Mark 14:21). Judas fulfilled Scripture and set up the centerpiece of God's redemptive plan, and yet Jesus said that the punishment for Judas' sinful actions was unparalleled.

Similarly, those who angrily called for Jesus' crucifixion were clearly playing right into God's good plan to redeem us from the penalty of our sins. And while Peter called these men "lawless" and appealed to them to "repent" of this horrible evil, he also said in the same sermon that this was all "according to the definite plan and foreknowledge of God" (Acts 2:23, 38).

That these sins, or any others, are justifiably punishable by God and yet at the same time all a part of God's sovereign plan is admittedly a difficult set of truths. But these truths both sit contentedly side by side in the Bible. They are, as Don Carson says, a "tension" that cannot be swept under the carpet. He reminds us,

> There is no escape from the sovereignty-responsibility tension, except by moving so far from the biblical data that either the picture of God or the picture of man bears little resemblance to their portraits as assembled from the scriptural texts themselves. It is no answer to tell me that my presentation of the sovereignty-responsibility tension still embraces certain unresolved tensions. Of course it does. But to correct me you must not claim to resolve all the tensions, for such a delusion is easily exposed. Rather, if you wish to convince me that your theology in this matter is more essentially Christian than

my own, you must show me how your shaping of the tension better conforms to the biblical data than mine does.[1]

It is sufficient, then, for Christians to affirm that God is sovereign over the events of life and human history, and yet those who choose to do what is evil will be held accountable for their actions.

2. Sin Is Always Sinful

There is an old story of a man who, when returning from church, was asked what the sermon was about. The man simply replied, "Sin." When asked what the preacher said about sin, the man answered, "He was against it." Not a bad synopsis of what I hope is still carried out of church by those who hold a high view of God's sovereignty. No matter how we see God using evil for good, let us all reaffirm that God, the Bible, and (I hope!) all Christians are against sin.

One reason we should loathe sin is because the Bible tells us it brings pain to God's heart. Remember that our experience with emotions is a reflection of the capacity that our Creator possesses. He feels pain, grief, and sorrow. And he has told us that the things that cause him pain are the sinful decisions of human beings. After describing the continual evil in the thoughts and intentions of people's hearts, the Bible tells us that "it grieved him [God] to his heart" (Genesis 6:6). Even the just punishment that is rightly given out by God is something that pains the Lord's emotions (Ezekiel 33:11; Luke 13:34-35).

Just the thought of God's promise to judge sin ought to safeguard us from ever being tolerant of it in our minds and lives. At the end of the book of Ecclesiastes, Solomon writes,

> The end of the matter; all has been heard. Fear God and keep his commandments, for this is the whole duty of man. For God will bring every deed into judgment, with every secret thing, whether good or evil (Ecclesiastes 12:13-14).

While Christ's work on behalf of his children will free us from the eternal consequences of our sins, the Bible is clear that sin in the Christian's life is not without cost. Not only will we reap what we sow (Galatians 6:7), but the Bible also tells us that sinful decisions will cause us to "suffer loss" on the day of our accountability (1 Corinthians 3:13-15). In his letter to the Christians in Rome, Paul wrote, "We will all stand before the judgment seat of God" and that "each of us will give an account of himself to God" (Romans 14:10-12). This kind of accountability in our lives as Christians should prevent us from ever thinking that because God is sovereign over all things, and because he works all the bad out for our good, then doing wrong can't be all that bad. The truth is that doing wrong is bad, and we will regret the sinful choices we make.

Our expected view toward sin is aptly summed up by this practical encouragement from Peter:

> You are a chosen race, a royal priesthood, a holy nation, a people for his own possession, that you may proclaim the excellencies of him who called you out of darkness into his marvelous light. Once you were not a people, but now you are God's people; once you had not received mercy, but now you have received mercy.
>
> Beloved, I urge you as sojourners and exiles to abstain from the passions of the flesh, which wage war against your soul. Keep your conduct among the Gentiles honorable, so that when they speak against you as evildoers, they may see your good deeds and glorify God on the day of visitation (1 Peter 2:9-12).

3. Persuading People to Do Good Is Always Good

We need to maintain a zeal for calling people to avoid sin and to do good. Consider Moses sincerely pleading with Pharaoh to let the Israelites go, while at the same time behind the scenes we learn that God was sovereignly orchestrating this showdown with Egypt as a means to display his redemptive power (Romans 9:17). Yes, God was planning and working all of this for his good purpose, but what Pharaoh was doing was still wrong, and Moses was right to passionately plead with him to do what was right.

Titus was a pastor on the island of Crete, a place that was notorious for its sinful inhabitants. Paul urged him on in his work by conceding with the popular sentiment of the day that "Cretans are always liars, evil beasts, [and] lazy gluttons," but saying that because this "testimony is true" Titus should "rebuke them sharply, that they may be sound in the faith" (Titus 1:12-13). While Paul knew that "evil men and imposters will go on from bad to worse," he also said that the right thing for Christians to do is to continue to call people to do good (2 Timothy 3:13; 4:1-5).

If God weren't so gracious the problem of evil wouldn't exist, but neither would we.

The biblical analogy of light and darkness for the realities of sin and evil is carried into the repeated exhortation for us to remember our identity and our mission. Paul wrote:

> At one time you were darkness, but now you are light in the Lord. Walk as children of light (for the fruit of light is found in all that is good and right and true), and try to discern what is pleasing to the Lord. Take no part in the unfruitful works of darkness, but instead expose them. For it is shameful even to speak of the things that they do in secret. But when anything is exposed by the light, it becomes visible, for anything that becomes visible is light. Therefore it says, "Awake, O sleeper, and arise from the dead, and Christ will shine on you" (Ephesians 5:8-14).

Preaching, counseling, and calling people to do what is right are as appropriate as Christians proclaiming the gospel to a lost world. Yes, many will continue to do evil, and God will use their rebellion for his sovereign and good plan. But our responsibility is to call sinners to repentance and to persuade men and women to do good.

The Eradication of Evil

God's master plan is to one day eradicate evil without condemning all those who have done evil. That divine goal initiated a long and strategic path that ends with the coming of Christ, and will be followed by the ingathering of a family of redeemed men and women. In the meantime, above and over it all is an all-knowing, all-powerful, and all-good God, who has scheduled his adopted children to live for a time in a fallen world—filled with much suffering, pain, sin, and evil.

If God weren't so gracious the problem of evil wouldn't exist, but neither would we. So because of God's gracious redemptive plan, we will suffer for a season. And when we do, we should long even more for the coming deliverance of this world. Because of Christ, the victory over sin and suffering is certain. And therefore we should anxiously await God's good purpose to be realized for his creation.

As one theologian wrote back in 1936:

> Revelation and reason unite in one testimony that evil is a temporary thing in the universe of God. Reason declares that, since God is infinitely holy and the Designer and Creator of the Universe, evil must have begun its manifestation subsequent to creation and by His permission and is to serve a purpose compatible with His righteousness. Reason also anticipates that, when that purpose is accomplished, evil will be dismissed from the universe of God, and that God, having undertaken to deal with evil, will complete His task to that degree of perfection which characterizes all His works. On the other hand, revelation predicts a coming victory over evil which no unaided finite mind can grasp.[2]

CHAPTER 10

Reasons for Confidence
No Matter What

I can remember back to those late October evenings when as a child, I stood in long lines and gave up my hard-earned allowance so I could enter the local shopping center's haunted house. Looking back on it, I have no idea why I would have paid anything to be scared, spooked, or frightened. I have long since failed to find any amusement in having my emotions unnerved by gory things unexpectedly jumping out at me. Maybe one reason is because after so many years in pastoral ministry, I have discovered that everyone who truly suffers is plagued by a variety of unsettling feelings of vulnerability and uncertainty. And those haunting feelings are anything but amusing, and they aren't over in fifteen minutes like those experienced in a haunted house on Halloween.

As C.S. Lewis wrote upon the death of his wife, "No one ever told me that grief felt so like fear."[1] It is true. Our experiences of pain and suffering are usually accompanied by an onslaught of worry, anxiety, and fear. When the familiarity of our health, relationships, or finances is taken away, not only do we hurt, but we also naturally experience the fear and insecurity of loss.

God on Fear and Anxiety

If we are familiar with the teaching of Christ, then we should immediately recognize the incompatibility of words like *fear*, *anxiety*, *worry*, and *insecurity* with Christianity. The Bible has a lot to say about these crippling emotions and how we should always seek to combat them. How often did Jesus say, "Fear not" (Luke 12:7) and "Do not be anxious about your life" (Matthew 6:25)? The Bible even goes so far as to say, "Do not be anxious about anything" (Philippians 4:6). And yet our hearts seem hopelessly overpowered by these strong feelings when the circumstances in our lives go seriously wrong.

At first glance, all these commands regarding our emotions seem unreasonable. How can God tell us to stop feeling a certain way? Who can just snap their fingers and obediently change their emotional state? Obviously God realizes that these feelings spring from the conditions we are facing. But he also knows that these emotions are products of our thinking in response to those conditions. That is why all these biblical commands regarding our emotions are found in contexts that address our thoughts.

> Our feelings will lie to us. God will not.

We may rightly argue that we cannot just snap our fingers and change the way we feel, but we must also admit that we possess the dignity endowed to all human beings of being able to direct and adjust our thoughts. God would have us endure our current trials without fear, insecurity, worry, and apprehension. To do so, we have to think right thoughts—thoughts that correspond to the truth. Our feelings will lie to us. God will not.

Before we consider the various adjustments we need to make in our thinking when we suffer, let's find out why, according to the Bible, we would naturally be tempted with these disquieting emotions.

The Evil in the Pain

When David poetically depicted the suffering in his life, he wrote the familiar words, "Even though I walk through the valley of the shadow of death, I will fear no evil" (Psalm 23:4). This connection between the things that cause pain and the evil David resolves not to fear is an important relationship to understand. Whether we are walking through the shadow of death, sickness, loss, injustice, harassment, or some other form of attack, we should take a moment to consider its connection to evil—which is inherently frightening.

Jesus said of Satan, "The thief comes only to steal and kill and destroy" (John 10:10). Earlier in the same Gospel he said, "The devil…was a murderer from the beginning" (8:44). The writer of Hebrews tells us that Jesus came to "destroy the one who has the power of death, that is, the devil" (Hebrews 2:14). Christ and the apostles repeatedly refer to the devil as "the evil one." He is the embodiment of evil, and he seeks to hurt, injure, steal, and destroy.

As we saw in the account of Job, though God carefully managed all that happened in the course of his suffering, the direct agents of all that went wrong in Job's life were Satan and his demonic henchmen. Consider again some of the specific things that brought Job such great pain: First, it was a band of crooks—the marauding Sabeans who stole all of his possessions (1:14-15). But, as Job 1:12 states, this was the strategic work of the evil one himself.

Next it was the natural disasters of what some might call "wicked weather" that destroyed his flocks (1:16). But, as we know, Satan was behind it all, working deliberately to take what Job owned.

Then it was the death of his children. As we saw above, death is the domain of the enemy.

Next, Job's pain came via an excruciating illness (2:7). Again, we were forewarned that this is the work of the destroyer.

Last, and for much of the rest of the book, it can be argued that the discouragement, bad advice, and false teaching Job encountered from his wife and friends can be directly attributed to the "liar and the father of lies," as Jesus said (John 8:44). The evil one and false teaching have always gone hand in hand (Revelation 16:13).

Yes, God is sovereign over it all, both in Job's life and in ours. And yes, Satan is not allowed to do more than what God permits. But it is important to recognize that when Job encountered all the "wrong" he experienced, and when we encounter all the "wrong" in our lives, we are actually experiencing the work of the evil one. Just acknowledging this reality can send a chill down our spine. These "bad things" are inherently evil, and regardless of the human or bacterial agency, they all—in one way or another—come from the hand of the evil one.

God Is on Our Side

While the thought of the evil one having an effect on our lives is enough to invoke a good deal of fear and dread, the Bible says we can and should be fearless in the face of such attacks—because there is someone greater on our side. Paul wrote to the first-century Roman Christians who were facing all sorts of tribulations, distresses, and persecutions and asked the rhetorical question, "If God is for us, who can be against us?" (Romans 8:31). Whenever I read that question I always think that the Roman Christians could have constructed a lot of answers—which were ultimately tied to the demon opponents of God. And Paul knew they had a long list of adversaries. He even provided a comprehensive list in the following verses. And he was careful to include not only the physical issues of famine and the government's sword, but also the driving force behind them, namely the fallen "angels," spiritual "rulers," and demonic "powers" (verses 35-38).

The logic here, of course, is that God is far greater than all of our spiritual enemies. Rightly understanding that fact can alleviate our fears and dispel our anxieties. As John later wrote when discussing the spiritual forces that work against us, "Little children, you are from God and have overcome them, for he who is in you is greater than he who is in the world" (1 John 4:4). The spiritual enemies of God, who love to "steal and kill and destroy," are admittedly menacing. But they have all been sentenced at the first coming of Christ and will all be condemned at his second coming. As Martin Luther put it in his famous hymn of 1529:

> And though this world, with devils filled,
> should threaten to undo us,
> We will not fear, for God hath willed
> His truth to triumph through us:
> The Prince of Darkness grim,
> we tremble not for him;
> His rage we can endure,
> for lo, his doom is sure,
> One little word shall fell him.
> That word above all earthly powers.[2]

With a word, Christ will bring an end to all the hostile spiritual forces of evil that have harassed and afflicted his children through the ages. The victory has been won at the cross and it is only a matter of time until, with a single word, Jesus will bring their evil work to an end. If you are a Christian, then the all-powerful triune God is on your side. You are on the winning team. And though the forces of evil continue to battle against all that is good in your world and in your life, there is coming a day when Christ will exercise his great power and right every wrong.

This is a perspective that changes the inner turmoil that often accompanies our painful trials. Remember how Christ slept in the boat during the storm on the Sea of Galilee? A confidence in the all-powerful God and the thought of our future deliverance can calm our hearts long before our storm is calmed. The Old Testament hymnal put it like this:

> For the righteous will never be moved;
> he will be remembered forever.
> He is not afraid of bad news;
> his heart is firm, trusting in the LORD.
> His heart is steady; he will not be afraid,
> until he looks in triumph on his adversaries (Psalm
> 112:6-8).

May God grant you a steady heart in the midst of the evil you face—whether it is the reality of death, the pain of discord, or the crush of some other oppression. This trust and firmness of heart is the daily goal for my own family as we face the variety of effects from Stephanie's disabilities. Her impaired mobility, her daily urinary and gastrointestinal challenges, and the variety of necessary medical devices and medications remind us of the far-reaching impact of the enemy's work. Yet we choose to trust in our sovereign God and refuse to be disheartened by the latest bad news regarding her condition. We have decided to "not be afraid" until we look in triumph on our adversaries. That, we are confident, will come with the resurrected and glorified body that Jesus promised.

The Pressing Needs

Reminding ourselves of the promised long-term outcome for our daughter's disability can bring us assurance and confidence, but many of the temptations to worry and fret come from the short-term battles. It's the besetting infections, surgical complications, painful therapies, needed orthotics, and the continual battle with insurance coverage (when the only pediatric neurosurgeon in the county is now suddenly *out of network*). It is when the constant catheterizations and frequent infections are threatening permanent kidney damage—it's these things that can set off a fierce battle with worry and fear.

I know this is the case with most trials. The daily needs and demands are often overwhelming. We can rest in the long-term outcome, but what about the pressing needs we face right now? As we endure all the demanding challenges of our current trial, we should remember Christ's continual exhortation to get our *needs* in perspective. I can sympathize with the loud clamor of today's urgent needs, but as Jesus said, there is not an earthly threat that should produce any real fear in the hearts of those who are rightly related to God. On the surface this may seem unattainable, but Jesus said, "Do not fear those who [can] kill the body" (Matthew 10:28). That is usually where all my temporal fears end. I suppose it is the same with you.

Consider what would happen in the worst-case scenario. Suppose none of the urgent needs raised in your trial were met. What would be the result if the things you feared and worried about actually happened? Many times it would mean more pain, greater suffering, mounting financial burdens, or perhaps even death. Even in that scenario, Jesus said, "Don't worry!" In the rest of Matthew 10:28, Jesus said our only real fear should be of "him who can destroy both soul and body in hell." That should serve as a wake-up call! The needs we face, even the most urgent ones, can't bring the threat of eternal condemnation. Jesus goes on to say that if you've made peace with the One who can cast you into hell, then anything less is not worth worrying about. He compares us to the birds over which the Lord exercises care and for which he actively provides. He then commands us: "Fear not, therefore; you are of more value than many sparrows" (verse 31).

This was the perspective that drove the fearlessness of Shadrach, Meshach, and Abednego. Remember their resolve to do right under the threat of Nebuchadnezzar's fiery furnace? They clearly had a pressing need. As bad as it was, the worst the king could do was kill them. They asserted their confidence that God could save them, and even a sense that God would. "But if not," they said, we are still going to trust him with our lives (Daniel 3:16-18).

God's Promised Provision

Once we get our *pressing needs* in perspective, Christ instructs us to have confidence that God cares for us in the midst of our situation. And though, under the sovereign watch of God, even the lives of birds come to a providential end, his pattern is to generously provide for his own. God has not promised to exempt us from suffering, but his track record is to generously give to his children in the midst of their struggles.

As Paul goes on to tell the suffering Christians in Rome, "He who did not spare his own Son but gave him up for us all, how will he not also with him graciously give us all things?" (Romans 8:32). Think about the argument being made with that statement. God demonstrated his generous love toward us in that he supplied for our critical need by paying the ultimate price of having his Son serve as the sin offering for our transgressions. If God did not hold back that invaluable gift, Paul argues, then why should we doubt that he would lovingly provide us with whatever else we need amid our trials?

If you study the historical context of some of Christ's most reassuring words regarding the Father's provision, you will discover that within a few decades, the audiences who heard Christ preach, "Do not be anxious about your life, what you will eat or what you will drink, nor about your body, what you will put on" were going to endure some terrible times under the persecution of the Roman Empire (Matthew 6:25). A Roman general was going to sweep through the land and wreak havoc on the nation of Israel. Their freedoms would be lost and their lands would be seized. They were going to face some extremely tough times—especially those who had stepped up to follow Christ. And yet with all of that on the horizon, Jesus emphatically said:

> Look at the birds of the air: they neither sow nor reap nor gather into barns, and yet your heavenly Father feeds them. Are you not of more value than they? And which of you by being anxious can add a single hour to his span

of life? And why are you anxious about clothing? Consider the lilies of the field, how they grow: they neither toil nor spin, yet I tell you, even Solomon in all his glory was not arrayed like one of these. But if God so clothes the grass of the field, which today is alive and tomorrow is thrown into the oven, will he not much more clothe you, O you of little faith? Therefore do not be anxious, saying, "What shall we eat?" or "What shall we drink?" or "What shall we wear?" For the Gentiles seek after all these things, and your heavenly Father knows that you need them all. But seek first the kingdom of God and his righteousness, and all these things will be added to you (Matthew 6:26-33).

The storms were sure to come, but the people were to remain calm, trust in God's goodness, seek first his priorities, and watch how he would provide. And as it was with Shadrach, Meshach, and Abednego, so we must be ready to trust God even if the worst-case scenario plays out. But as most of us can attest, God usually reaches out in the course of our trial and provides just what is needed—often in the eleventh hour, and often in ways that are different than requested. Yet as Christ stated in Matthew 6, God always does this with an intimate interest in and concern for all that we need.

Jesus diagnosed our problem and identified the source of our worry as a lack of faith in the care of our "heavenly Father." In other words, we fail to have the trust that young children have in the provisions of their earthly fathers. Picture a dad pulling out of the driveway with his children. How often do the little kids start to worry and ask questions like, "Dad, are you sure we have enough gas to get where we are going?" "Are our insurance premiums paid up on the car?" "Do you have enough money in your wallet for lunch?" "Dad, when was the last time you checked the tire pressure, or got

> Our Father in heaven knows what we need. Let's not worry.

the oil changed?" No, they just settle in and wonder how long it will take to get there. They trust their dad to get them to where they need to go. They are confident in their father's care and have no concern for car maintenance, driving directions, or cash on hand.

Of course good dads never promote negligence or irresponsibility in their children. I always run through a quick checklist before I drive off in the car with my kids. I ask, "Do you have your wallets?" "Did you bring your backpacks?" But even so, my kids know that if they run out of allowance money or have a genuine need, dad is there—they are not alone. And neither are we. As God's children, we should have that sense of security, well-being, and protection that is the product of our genuine trust in the care and provision of our heavenly Father

Our Father in heaven knows what we need. Let's not worry. Whatever the related concerns are that have come with our current crisis, let us exchange our anxiety for prayer. Philippians 4 says that when you "let your requests be made known to God," you will experience "the peace of God, which surpasses all understanding" (verses 6-7).

Guilt in the Pain

Worse than being worried by our pressing needs, or frightened by the palpable activity of the evil one in our trials, can be the haunting sense of guilt that often permeates our seasons of suffering. I am not talking about the proper introspection that seeks to discover whether our encounter with pain is actually God's corrective discipline. I am referring to a kind of guilt that can preoccupy us even when our suffering has nothing at all to do with divine correction.

It is hard for me to overstate how often I see Christians end up wallowing in guilt and self-reproach as they go through difficult times. Perhaps you have felt yourself being drawn toward feelings of regret and remorse even though you have confidently ruled out any connection between some personal sin and your painful circumstances. It happens all the time.

Remember that the death of Job's children, his financial collapse, and all his health problems had nothing to do with some secret sin or unconfessed transgression. And yet it didn't take long for Job to tailspin into a depressive self-loathing. Not only did he curse the day of his birth (Job 3:1-10) and fall into hating himself (10:1-3), but he began to see his incredibly painful trial as God's way to get back at him for the things he had done as a teenager. He became convinced that God hated him (16:9). Job wrongly said of God:

> Why do you hide your face and count me as your enemy?...For you write bitter things against me and make me inherit the iniquities of my youth. You put my feet in the stocks and watch all my paths (Job 13:24, 26-27).

Nothing could have been further from the truth. Do you remember how the book of Job began? God was bragging about Job to the evil one:

> The LORD said to Satan, "Have you considered my servant Job, that there is none like him on the earth, a blameless and upright man, who fears God and turns away from evil?" (Job 1:8)

Obviously God knew of Job's inherent weaknesses and his less-than-perfect life. Yes, God knew of all the sins of Job's youth, and every other transgression Job had ever committed. But none of that was on God's mind. As it is with us, God graciously forgives and pardons the contrite sinner. He had also empowered Job to live an exemplary life and faithfully pursue righteousness. This terrible season of Job's life had nothing to do with Job's sin, and yet Job was drowning in the guilt and memories of his past wrongdoings.

Promoting this *false* guilt is a common tactic of the enemy. He would love to see you follow in Job's footsteps by having you find an unreasonable and unfounded connection from your imperfect life to the death of your loved one, your ongoing infertility, your financial struggles, or your cancer diagnosis. If you have adequately invited God's Spirit to search your heart, as we described in chapter 2, and you have no reasonable conviction that your current crisis is God's loving discipline for some unforsaken sin, then you are being trapped. Watch out! Don't fall for the enemy's tactics.

Perfectly Loved and Forgiven

Not only does God want us to be fearless when we experience the effects of the evil one in our trials and endure our crises without worry even in the face of pressing needs, but God desires for us to endure our seasons of suffering free from guilt.

Here's how Paul reassured the first-century Christians suffering in Rome:

> Who shall bring any charge against God's elect? It is God who justifies. Who is to condemn? Christ Jesus is the one who died—more than that, who was raised—who is at the right hand of God, who indeed is interceding for us (Romans 8:33-34).

Don't lose sight of the setting for these words. Paul was addressing those going through "tribulation," "distress," "persecution," "famine," "danger," and the "sword" of their oppressors (verse 35). This reassurance regarding Christ's intercession for us is often considered out of context. The reason this truth is so necessary in Paul's flow of thought in Romans 8 is because suffering regularly ensnares Christians with feelings of being *charged* and *condemned* (verse 33). In this passage the Bible is getting us to reaffirm the fact that even during the darkest trials of our lives we can have the full confidence that the only one who can truly condemn or charge us is the One who has become our Redeemer and Advocate.

Six centuries before Christ, after a portion of the Israelites held captive in Babylon had returned to their land, Zechariah recorded a vision of their new high priest. His name was Joshua, and like his namesake from the days of Moses, we can assume he did not become the high priest by being a spiritual or moral slacker. In Zechariah 3 we read of this spiritual and religious leader being accused by *Satan*— by the way, the devil's name means "one who accuses." The response of the angel of the Lord is, in essence, "I know Joshua is an imperfect sinner who is a product of grace" (verse 2). But then an amazing picture unfolds, one that reads like a New Testament text about our standing in Christ. The angel in this vision commands that the high priest's "filthy garments" be removed and that he be clothed in "pure vestments" (verse 4). Satan is rebuked, and Joshua is dressed in clean clothes that are not his own.

> We must endure our tough times with the bold confidence that we are perfectly loved and accepted by God.

It is hard to find a better picture of our forgiveness and justification through Jesus Christ, which the New Testament later describes as our being *clothed in him* (Galatians 3:27). We are accepted, favored, embraced, and deeply loved by the Father because of the righteousness of Christ. As John wrote:

> My little children, I am writing these things to you so that you may not sin. But if anyone does sin, we have an advocate with the Father, Jesus Christ the righteous. He is the propitiation for our sins, and not for ours only but also for the sins of the whole world (1 John 2:1-2).

When we are suffering, we need to be reminded that our pain is not necessarily a sign that God is against us or *hates us,* as Job had wrongly concluded in his case. In spite of all the discomforts of our trial, God accepts us because of Christ. Our sins have been covered by his death. Jesus became the *propitiation* or the satisfaction for all that our sins and transgressions required from a holy and just Judge. We must endure our tough times with the bold confidence that we are perfectly loved and accepted by God. We must shun the tempting thoughts that somehow our pain is God's divine payback. We have to fight these thoughts because the Bible could not be clearer—there is "no condemnation for those who are in Christ Jesus" (Romans 8:1). You may not yet know the *good* that God is working in the bad you are experiencing, but if you are a Christian, don't ever fall into the enemy's trap of thinking that your pain is a sign that your heavenly Father has aligned himself against you. God couldn't be any more for you than he has proved to be by the sacrifice of his Son.

Living Fearlessly

Fear, anxiety, worry, and insecurity will be perpetual temptations—especially as we walk through the various shadowy valleys our Good Shepherd has purposed to lead us through. Even so, may we be resolved not to fear, but instead, to cling to Christ with a deepening and abiding trust.

Like Shadrach, Meshach, and Abednego, David knew what it was to trust God when confronted with scary and intimidating threats. One of the daunting *shadows* David faced as a young man was Goliath's. This tyrant could have easily snuffed out the young shepherd boy's life. But instead of cowering, David placed his faith squarely in God. Listen to his words as he approached his opponent:

> You come to me with a sword and with a spear and with a javelin, but I come to you in the name of the LORD of hosts, the God of the armies of Israel, whom you have defied (1 Samuel 17:45).

Your trial may seem as ominous as a fiery furnace or as enormous as an oversized Philistine warrior. Even so, God is calling you to faith, not fear. The Lord would have you trust that he is greater than any foe you face. Your Father wants you to be confident that he can and will provide for your needs. The Savior would have you wholeheartedly believe that he is for you and not against you.

Believe him!

CHAPTER 11

God's Unchanging Love
in a Turbulent World

When I was a kid, there were times when my dad would say to me, "You're skating on thin ice!" Having been raised in sunny Southern California, I had never actually had the experience of skating on thin ice. In fact, I'm not sure I had ever put on a pair of ice skates during the years when I heard that familiar phrase. But I can assure you that I got the point! Dad wanted me to know I had done something that had landed me in a precarious situation. In my early years this meant the well-being of my posterior was suddenly at risk. Later, as a teenager, it meant that my hopes for fulfilling my weekend plans were suddenly in jeopardy.

As adults we have all experienced the feeling of living life on *thin ice*. As grown-ups, we may prefer phrases like "the bottom is falling out of my financial situation," "my marriage is collapsing," "my health is falling apart," or "my work situation is disintegrating." But we all know what it is like to live with uncertainty. We have all faced an unexpected turn of events that dashed our sense of stability, peace, and security in every area of life. Every area, that is, except one! While every single thing in life may be subject to change, disruption, and collapse, for the Christian there is one huge exception—our relationship with God.

The Bible tells Christians that because of the nature of God's love for us, which is unlike any earthly love we've ever experienced, we can be certain that God's loyalty, care, and concern for us is unchanging. This truth was vividly portrayed throughout many of the Old Testament psalms when the suffering saints described the Lord as their Rock and their Fortress. Repeatedly, though armies were attacking or some other trouble was pressing in on them, they came back to describing their relationship with God as the stable, secure, and enduring shelter to which they could run.

We can modernize the ancient images of the rock and fortress by picturing our Christian lives as walking on the deck of a Nimitz-class aircraft carrier, which is reinforced with multiple layers of steel plates. We may be navigating the roughest seas of our lives over shark-infested waters, but our lives are buoyed by 500 tons of aluminum and 47,000 tons of steel. The aircraft carrier of God's love, which is the foundation of our relationship with the Lord, will not give way just because we encounter some unexpected turbulence. Regardless of the tough times in life, we can possess incomprehensible peace and incomparable security because God's love is infinitely better and completely unlike any other love on planet earth.

God's Faithful Love

At age thirteen I was told by my friend, who was told by another friend, who was told by still another friend, that Jennifer (a pretty seventh-grade girl) *liked* me. I was ecstatic. I quickly sent word back through the *love chain* that I also *liked* her very much. My friend told his friend, who told his other friend, who told her friend, who then delivered my message to her. Two days later, as I was planning our life together,

> God's love is different. It is not based on the shifting emotions of the human heart.

a message came back through the *love chain* that she didn't like me anymore.

I wish I could say, "So goes the fickle 'love' of junior-highers." But I realize this situation is not all that different from the so-called love most people experience well beyond middle school. "Many a man proclaims his own steadfast love," the Bible says, "but a faithful man who can find?" (Proverbs 20:6). You will encounter a lot of people in this life who will profess their commitment to you, say they will always stand with you, and loyally be there for you, who only end up walking away never to return.

God's love is different. It is not based on the shifting emotions of the human heart. When the God of the Bible chooses to set his love on his children, his unchanging nature ensures that there is nothing fickle or indecisive about his commitment to us. No amount of time and no circumstances can change that. Paul could not have stated it more emphatically:

> Who shall separate us from the love of Christ? Shall tribulation, or distress, or persecution, or famine, or nakedness, or danger, or sword? As it is written, "For your sake we are being killed all the day long; we are regarded as sheep to be slaughtered." No, in all these things we are more than conquerors through him who loved us. For I am sure that neither death nor life, nor angels nor rulers, nor things present nor things to come, nor powers, nor height nor depth, nor anything else in all creation, will be able to separate us from the love of God in Christ Jesus our Lord (Romans 8:35-39).

Ponder that promise. God's love is faithful and loyal. Nothing can separate us from it. Paul knew the Christians he was writing to were both suffering and under attack, but his assurance to them was that even if their temporal circumstances were as bad as they could possibly be, God's love for them would never be withdrawn. So it is for us. If every last person were to turn away from us, and all the forces of hell seemed as though they were pitted against us, God's love would remain constant. He "will never leave you or forsake you" (Hebrews 13:5).

God's All-Powerful Love

At age seventeen, in a day before cell phones, text messaging, and emails, I packed up my belongings in a duffle bag, said good-bye to my girlfriend, and traveled 2000 miles from home to begin my college education in Chicago. There were plenty of doubts as to whether our high school love could survive the dreaded *long-distance dating* relationship. We knew that the extreme distance, the challenge of communication, the extended time away from each other, along with a variety of other distractions, would be a genuine threat to our young love.

God boldly promises his faithful love to us even though the problems and challenges of life pose a seemingly endless series of threats to that love. Can God's love for us really endure this problem, that crisis, today's disappointment, and tomorrow's failure? It is easy to doubt. But unlike the young love of a couple of teenagers, the powerful love of God should never be called into question. Romans 8:35-39 lists a variety of painful and powerful threats—things like tribulation, persecution, swords, angels, rulers, and death, among other things. The Bible's response to those assaults is that *nothing* "in all creation, will be able to separate us from the love of God in Christ Jesus our Lord" (verse 39).

That is not romantic hyperbole. God can back it up. There is not enough combined power in all the universe to ever truly threaten the all-powerful God and his decisive commitment of love to his children. There may be a lot of terrible circumstances that tempt us to question God's love, but as the cross of Christ proved, his decision to love his people is eternally settled, and nothing can separate us from that relationship. As Jesus said,

> I give them eternal life, and they will never perish, and
> no one will snatch them out of my hand. My Father,
> who has given them to me, is greater than all, and no one
> is able to snatch them out of the Father's hand. I and the
> Father are one (John 10:28-30).

God's love demonstrated to us in the life, death, and resurrection of Christ should forever resolve the matter in our hearts. There is not a problem, a catastrophe, a threat, or a tragedy that could ever drive a wedge between God and his dearly loved people.

I realize that teenage love is not worthy to be compared to God's love, but I am nevertheless encouraged by the way God displayed his grace in allowing my high school girlfriend to become my wife after my college studies in Chicago were completed. The many challenges of our long-distance relationship were overcome by our imperfect reflection of those divine commitments, which are all perfectly demonstrated for us in Christ. God's eternally strong love for us will never be overpowered by life's uncertainties or the troubles we encounter from year to year. Trust God. Hang on. Put your confidence in his unquenchable and all-powerful love.

God's All-Knowing Love

There are times in the life of every parent when a sincere promise is made to our children to do this or that, or go here or there, but then some unforeseen circumstance arises that changes everything. "Yes, I know I said we'd have pizza on Saturday, but I didn't know we'd have guests from out of town." "Sure, I said I'd take you to the ball game on Thursday night, but I didn't know you'd be grounded." We can be heartfelt and completely sincere in our commitments only to watch them unravel because we cannot see the future. We can't possibly know all the variables that might derail our honest intentions.

Our limited knowledge concerning the future is the reason many human love relationships come to an end. We didn't know this or that *unlovable thing* about the person when we began to love them. We had no idea this person would do all these terrible things when we initially chose to love them. But God's love has no such limitation. Be sure to catch this huge difference between human love and divine love. God knows everything. He knows everything about you. He not only knows the depths of your thoughts and character right now, he perceives in vivid detail all the things you have yet to do in the future.

Ponder the incredible truths of Psalm 139. As you do, consider the fact that when God chose to love you and adopt you as his beloved child he knew you this thoroughly:

> O LORD, you have searched me and known me!
> You know when I sit down and when I rise up;
> you discern my thoughts from afar.
> You search out my path and my lying down
> and are acquainted with all my ways.
> Even before a word is on my tongue,
> behold, O LORD, you know it altogether...
> Where shall I go from your Spirit?
> Or where shall I flee from your presence?...
> If I say, "Surely the darkness shall cover me,
> and the light about me be night,"
> even the darkness is not dark to you;
> the night is bright as the day,
> for darkness is as light with you.
> For you formed my inward parts;
> you knitted me together in my mother's womb...
> My frame was not hidden from you,
> when I was being made in secret,
> intricately woven in the depths of the earth.
> Your eyes saw my unformed substance;
> in your book were written, every one of them,
> the days that were formed for me,
> when as yet there was none of them
> (verses 1-4, 7, 11-13, 15-16).

This is a life-changing truth: *There are no surprises with God!* He has always known everything about you. He knew exactly what you'd be going through right now. He knew how you would handle the pain and the pressure. He knew everything about the best of your deeds and the worst of your sins. And yet, with all of this knowledge—with his eyes wide open—he chose to set his love on you. That love is a commitment made by God with full, complete, and thorough knowledge. And it should remind you that his love is not given as a response to how lovable you are. This gracious and unearned love is granted to you just because God in his infinite mercy and kindness decided to give it.

When Moses was assuring the imperfect people of his day about the intelligent love of God, he said that they were God's "treasured possession" not because they were better, more impressive, or greater than any other group of people (they certainly were not). Rather, Moses told them it was "because the LORD loves you and is keeping the oath that he swore to your fathers" (Deuteronomy 7:6-8). Why did God love them? Because he loved them, and was keeping his promise to love them. Likewise, his all-knowing love is set on us not because of what he knows about us, but in spite of what he knows about us. That is a truth worth celebrating with full confidence and faith. God loves his people with a full knowledge and an unchangeable resolve.

God's Unchanging Love

Not only does God never gain new knowledge about us, he is also a God who has emphatically told us that he is not subject to change, variation, growth, or modification.

> God's decision to love you is rooted in an eternal character that never changes.

After the writer of Hebrews tells us that God will "never leave you nor forsake you" and that "we can confidently say, 'The Lord is my helper; I will not fear; what man can do to me?'" he goes on to remind us, "Jesus Christ is the same yesterday and today and forever" (13:5-8). The fact of God's unchanging character is critically important when we consider the stability and strength of God's love.

Our doubting minds might think, *God may have chosen to love me with full knowledge of my life, but perhaps in time he will change his mind about me.* That is an understandable thought given the fickle nature of human love. Some people, without any new information, decide to walk away from their relationships simply because they grow tired of the people they had once chosen to love. God is not subject to this kind of human boredom. God is immutable, unchanging, existing eternally without variation.

God's decision to love you is rooted in an eternal character that never changes. Notice how the psalmist connects the immutable nature of God with the relational security his people enjoy.

> Of old you laid the foundation of the earth, and the heavens are the work of your hands. They will perish, but you will remain; they will all wear out like a garment. You will change them like a robe, and they will pass away, but you are the same, and your years have no end. The children of your servants shall dwell secure; their offspring shall be established before you (Psalm 102:25-28).

We may be tempted to forsake our commitments and shift our affections based on our personal growth and character development, but for God this is impossible. When our spiritual enemy works to have us doubt God's love for us in the midst of our trials, we must be sure to counter those attacks on our faith by recounting the unchanging nature of God's character. He doesn't change, and neither does his love for his children.

God's Gracious Love

At some point during our season of suffering we are bound to interpret the pain as something deserved, and the love of God as something we don't deserve—even after we have ruled out the likelihood that our pain is an act of God's discipline in response to some specific sin. It may not be the first thought we have when life hurts, but after all the fleshly bouts with "Why me?" and "I don't deserve this," at some quiet moment during our suffering we are prone to reflect on our imperfection and unworthiness and say, "Maybe this is all a reflection of how God *really* feels about me."

This is a dangerous and unbiblical thought. And therefore it is not enough to just speak of God's all-knowing and unchanging love. We also need to be brought back to the profound basis of God's love—his grace. We have touched on this already, but let's go further and remember the fact that the Lord's love demonstrated to us in Christ was *all* of grace—undeserved, unmerited, unearned, and in many ways illogical.

Consider the extent to which the Bible goes to make this point. "Christ died for the ungodly" (Romans 5:6). "God shows his love for us in that while we were still sinners, Christ died for us" (verse 8). "While we were enemies we were reconciled to God by the death of his Son" (verse 10). Note that the most costly expression of God's love was carried out for us when we had nothing on our resume but the words "ungodly," "sinners," and "enemies." That important clarification in Romans 5 comes after the declaration that "God's love has been poured into our hearts" (verse 5). How important it is for us to continually recall that God's love and acceptance, so generously poured out on us, is not gained because we deserve it!

With that in mind we can admit that ultimately, as those who have sinned against God, we actually do deserve suffering, and we certainly do not deserve God's love. But for Christians, that is the illogical arrangement of God's incredible love. And because of that arrangement, your suffering is *not an expression of how God feels about you*, or *what he thinks of you*. His commitment to you is love, acceptance, and forgiveness. That should not be doubted because we are able to uncover in our minds a string of thoughts that remind us of our unworthiness. Of course we are unworthy of his love, but we have it anyway. No, we don't deserve his acceptance, but he has granted it to us anyhow. So then, keep your faith firmly planted in the astounding truth of God's gracious love.

God's Transforming Love

Any biblical discussion of God's love can elevate our confidence in God's character and boost our assurance that he loves like no other. But the utter uniqueness of his love can spark another cause for doubting. We all experience relationships as a two-way street. And God may enter into this relationship with a perfect and unrivaled quality of love, but what about us? Our love can't be anything like his, can it? His love may be faithful, all-powerful, all-knowing, unchanging, and gracious, but isn't our love weak, subject to fading, changing, or failing?

That question brings us to the most unique and mysterious aspects of divine love. God's redemptive love toward his adopted children always renovates, alters, and transforms the love of those he loves. In other words, the New Testament tells us that when God sets his love on his forgiven and reconciled people, his love produces a capacity, strength, and awakening to love him in return—a kind of love that we were incapable of before. His love transforms our lives *and* our ability to love him back.

And this is why, when I quoted Romans 5:5 earlier, I quoted only part of it: "God's love has been poured into our hearts..." Now let's look at the rest of the verse: "God's love has been poured into our hearts *through the Holy Spirit who has been given to us.*" When God pours his love into our hearts, it is done in and through the person of the Holy Spirit. Since New Testament times, a person has not been able to be a recipient of the redemptive love of God without also having the Holy Spirit take up residence in his or her life. And when the Holy Spirit invades a person's life, it is changed—including that person's capacity for loving God.

The Spirit always gets right to work in the life of any person who truly becomes a Christian. And the first thing on his list is love—literally! Galatians 5:22 says, "The fruit of the spirit is love, joy, peace, patience..." among other things. Unlike human relationships, when God enters into a love relationship with someone, he implants his own Spirit in that person's life. While there is plenty working against the love he is generating in us (as Galatians 5 goes on to describe), the Bible promises that God will succeed in producing an enduring love in the hearts of his children. We may not love him perfectly, but because of the abiding presence of the Holy Spirit in our lives, we can be sure that our love for God will always remain.

For those who have evidence of God's Spirit in their lives, there is no cause for doubting. Hebrews 3:6 tells us that "Christ is faithful over God's house...And we are his house if we hold fast our confidence and our boasting in our hope." Be sure to read that as it is written. We don't "become" his house if we hold fast our confidence. We "are" his house if we hold fast our confidence. This enduring love, confidence, and boasting in our hope is the evidence that God's Spirit is in us. The same theme is repeated later in Hebrews 3: "For we have come to share in Christ, if indeed we hold our original confidence firm to the end" (verse 14). Again, we don't "get to" share in Christ if we hold our original confidence firm to the end. Rather, we "have come to" share in Christ if we hold our original confidence firm to the end.

If we have responded to the gospel in repentance and faith, and we are seeing the evidence that God's Spirit has taken up residence in our lives, then we can be certain that his agenda in our hearts is to ensure that our love for him will grow, mature, and endure. It should go without saying that the process will have plenty of ups and downs, but we must continue to restate that we are not alone in this "two-way street" of a relationship. The Holy Spirit is in us, and he is active in nurturing, developing, and cultivating within us a lasting love for the God who loves us. We can and should continue to be confident in the Lord's transforming love.

Done with Doubting

The more we understand about the divine love God has for his children, the greater the impact on the way in which we navigate our pain. Certainly this incredible love that has been lavished upon us in Christ should help dispel our doubts. Our faith is founded not on our fickle feelings or our changing circumstances, but on the historic truths of God's Word—proved to us by the life, death, and resurrection of his Son. Doubt is the domain of our spiritual enemy.

> You can believe what God said and what Christ did to prove it, or you can listen to the Tempter.

Think back to the account of the Garden of Eden in Genesis 3 when Satan showed up to tempt Eve. The strategy was simple: *Get God's people to doubt God's statements of fact.* God was clear about the rules and arrangements for life in the Garden, and yet Eve fell to the opening pitch of our enemy, "Did God actually say...?" (verse 1). By injecting doubt that suggested God's words could not be trusted, the Tempter went on to appeal to what Eve saw, felt, and experienced (verse 6). If he could get her to put more emphasis on what she *felt* and less on what God *said*, then Satan could get Eve to abandon the path of righteousness and fall into costly, destructive, and dishonoring sins. Satan would love to do the same in your life.

You can endure your current trials with dignity, faith, and hope in God by keeping your focus on the truth of what God has said. The costly path of sin and compromise begins with doubt—doubt regarding God's faithful, powerful, and unchanging love for you. You can believe what God said and what Christ did to prove it, or you can listen to the Tempter, who craftily works to get you to dismiss God's truth based on what you are going through. Understand these well-worn strategies of Satan and choose to believe God regardless of the pain.

No Second-Guessing God

It is good to regularly remind ourselves that we are not God. That may sound like a silly, if not blasphemous thing to say, but if we listen for it, we can often hear ourselves saying things that make it sound as though we think we can do a better job than God is currently doing. How often in our complaints that rise from sufferings is there an accusation regarding God's management of things in our lives? *After all*, we think, *if I were choosing to love someone, I certainly wouldn't be doling out these kinds of painful experiences.*

At some point in our Christian life we have to learn to humbly stand in awe of God's inscrutable wisdom. *Inscrutable* is a word we might not use often, but it's a perfect word for describing many aspects of God's thought process. After a particularly perplexing section of Scripture in which the apostle Paul seeks to trace out why God does what he does, the apostle caps his discussion with this worshipful declaration:

> Oh, the depth of the riches and wisdom and knowledge of God! How unsearchable are his judgments and how inscrutable his ways! "For who has known the mind of the Lord, or who has been his counselor?" "Or who has given a gift to him that he might be repaid?" For from him and through him and to him are all things. To him be glory forever. Amen (Romans 11:33-36).

God is smarter than you and I. He has wise, thoughtful, intelligent reasons for doing what he does. We should readily admit that his plan for this world, your life, and mine is likely beyond our ability to fully comprehend. Furthermore, as Dr. Waltke bluntly puts it, "Simply because God has a plan does not mean that he necessarily has any intention of sharing it with you; as a matter of fact the message of Job is in part that the Lord in his sovereignty may allow terrible things to happen to you and you may never know why."[1] That may be tough to swallow, but it should serve as another reminder that God is God and we are not. It should keep us from questioning his infinite wisdom.

When life hurts, it is important to accept the logical truth that God has so clearly revealed: "As the heavens are higher than the earth, so are my ways higher than your ways and my thoughts than your thoughts" (Isaiah 55:9). That can come off sounding like a copout in the ears of those who have been told God loves them and yet they suffer. But it's not a copout. It's nothing more than the reasonable expectation we place on our young children when they question the wisdom of any number of things we parents thoughtfully choose to subject them to. For a Christian of any age or experience to choose to interrogate the eternal God for why he would allow this or that shows a need for perspective.

God loves us. And we have taken a brief look at the kind of incomparable love he has for us. Given the unchanging nature of this love, we should then proceed without any bitter second-guessing of his path for our lives. We should humbly accept it and praise him for his inscrutable decisions, careful to never suggest that we are capable of being his counselor.

The End of Fretting

Last, let me quickly address our need to be done with the attitude of being a lowly victim, wallowing in our pain, perturbed, and fretting over our persecuted life. An elevated view of God's love for us should overcome all such temptations. It's possible for us to avoid doubting, and even cease from questioning God, only to retreat into a *poor me* mentality that obviously fails to bring glory to God and certainly fails to honor the truths of Scripture.

As in many of the psalms, David, in Psalm 37, provides urgent instructions for those who are undergoing painful trials. He repeatedly calls the sufferer to refrain from *fretting* (verses 1, 7, 8). He admits, as we have frequently considered throughout this book, that the scoreboard may not currently reflect the promised outcome that God's beloved children win and the unrepentant evildoers lose. But calls for us to "trust him" (verse 5) and "wait for it."

> Be still before the LORD and wait patiently for him; fret not yourself over the one who prospers in his way, over the man who carries out evil devices! Refrain from anger, and forsake wrath! Fret not yourself; it tends only to evil. For the evildoers shall be cut off, but those who wait for the LORD shall inherit the land (Psalm 37:7-9).

Waiting is hard. Waiting *well* is really hard. But our faith in the enduring, powerful love of God, which assures us of our final vindication and our coming redemption, can help us to wait well. Considering the eternal advantages of God's faithful love can help us to say with the rest of the psalm, "Better is the little that the righteous has than the abundance of many wicked" (verse 16). Who can argue with the fact that it is far better to have the love of God, along with all of our troubles, losses, diseases, and disasters, than to avoid them all and live as God's enemy? We can be confident that "the arms of the wicked shall be broken, but the LORD upholds the righteous. The LORD knows the days of the blameless, and their heritage will remain forever; they are not put to shame in evil times; in the days of famine they have abundance" (verses 17-19).

We may not feel rich in the depths of our suffering, but as the objects of God's amazing love we truly have an invaluable abundance. This needs to be our focus and the cause of our rejoicing. It should be the motivation for our thoughts and deeds to "turn away from evil and do good" because "he will not forsake his saints" (verses 27-28). So "wait for the LORD and keep his way" for "the salvation of the righteous is from the LORD; he is their stronghold in the time of trouble" (verses 34, 39). It may feel turbulent for us right now, but we are on anything but thin ice. God is our stronghold, our fortress, and our aircraft carrier deck.

Real Confidence

Speaking of turbulence, on a recent trip to San Francisco I was reminded just how tumultuous the ocean can be. My family and I stood on Crissy Field in the shadow of the towering Golden Gate Bridge. The wind was howling, as it often does there, and the white-caps on the bay could be seen in every direction. With wide eyes my wife brought up what it must have been like to be a construction worker on that mammoth project.

Indeed, the truth is that the prospect of building the 4200-foot-long suspension bridge in 1933 was daunting. In those days, the grim rule of thumb for bridge construction was the expectation of one lost life for every million dollars spent. The bids to erect the Golden Gate Bridge were coming in at $100 million dollars. Based on the rule of thumb, that's a lot of funerals for construction workers.

Bridge builder Joseph Strauss stepped up with an economical bid and a novel focus on safety. After seeing twenty-six lives lost on the construction of Oakland's Bay Bridge, Strauss approached this new project with sweeping mandatory safety measures, the center-piece of which was an astronomically expensive safety net. At the time, a $135,000 net seemed extravagant. And it was. But it saved many lives! When the gusty blasts of the San Francisco bay jetti-soned another worker off the scaffolding, it simply pitched him into the ever-present safety net.

The unforeseen byproduct of Strauss' life-saving safety net was a radical change in the minds and hearts of his workers. When the builders knew they were enveloped in a net that would always be there for their protection and deliverance, they tackled the chal-lenges and hazards of their dangerous jobs with a new sense of confidence, courage, and peace of mind. They worked better, faster, and more efficiently. And believe it or not, the entire project actually finished ahead of schedule and under budget!

Much like Strauss to those workers, I can't promise you there won't be problems, hassles, setbacks, pains, fatigue, and injuries. But I can assure you that in the Christian life we have a fortress, an anchor, a rock, a spiritual fleet of aircraft carriers, and an ever-present safety net in the love of God. His love envelops his children. God's divine love for his people is a stronghold for each of us in our time of trouble.

CHAPTER 12

Indispensable Resources for Life's Trials

It's been twelve years since that startling day in the obstetrician's office when the ultrasound gave us our first glimpse into the divinely ordained challenges Stephanie and the rest of our family would be facing. Surgeries, therapies, leg braces, catheters, wheelchairs, and a set of daily medical routines have become a familiar part of our lives ever since. By God's grace our daughter, along with every member of our family, continues to grow and mature in her understanding of how God uses suffering, setbacks, and painful episodes in life for the glory of Christ and the good of his church. One of the things we have all learned in this prolonged trial is the importance of some daily spiritual investments—investments that make a huge difference in how well we navigate this path.

Jesus once said, "Do not be anxious about tomorrow...Sufficient for the day is its own trouble" (Matthew 6:34). I realize, as Christ tells us, that speculating about the potential problems of the future is not helpful, and it's not hard to understand that yesterday is gone and all the "should haves" and "could haves" don't do us any good. The focus for you and me has to be on today and what we might do to best position ourselves for God to take us through our season of suffering.

A few basic spiritual investments are regularly neglected when Christians hurt—and when they are, it only makes things worse! God has prescribed these spiritual practices for all Christians, not only when things are going well, but also when things don't feel good. As a matter of fact, it seems that these foundational spiritual exercises of the Christian life play an even more critical role in our lives when the pressure is on and the pain is intense.

Get in Church

I can totally sympathize with the desire to withdraw when we enter a difficult season of life. I know what it's like to want to draw the shades and get through the day with the least amount of contact with others as possible. But we need to remember that the church, its people, and our participation with them are not optional. The New Testament spills a lot of ink describing how the church should be structured, how it is to function, what its purpose ought to be, and who should lead in it. God didn't go to all that trouble and give us numerous commands to get involved—only to let us opt out when life hurts. Christ designed the church for us and he expects us to be an integral part of it. We have to fight the tendency to step back or step out when we encounter serious pain in our lives. We can't afford to circle the wagons and only associate with a few close friends and family when we are struggling. This is a huge—and common—mistake.

We may be tempted to pull back from going to church when we are hurting because our church appears to be a "happy" gathering of "joyful" Christians who have it all together. Having been a pastor for many years I can attest that such assumptions are way off. And church is precisely where we need to be in pain-filled times. We need to get back to the biggest issues of life—our great God, our eternal salvation, and the organization Christ founded, which he promised the gates of hell would not prevail against (Matthew 16:18). Side by side with our brothers and sisters in Christ, worshipping and listening to the Word taught is right where we need to be.

When we stay involved in church our perspective will be broadened. Being there will get us to see that there is more going on in our world than just our personal pain. And when we really get involved with a servant's heart, it won't take long to recognize that there are other Christians in our midst who are facing even bigger and more painful struggles than we are. How helpful it can be to see that our church is not only filled with happy and joyful Christians, but is also, at any given time, filled with a number of hurting people in need of our care, support, and prayers. We may not feel like helping others, but watch what God will do in our own lives when, in our pain, we choose to come alongside a fellow believer who is hurting and in need of care.

In the Bible passage that tells us not to join in with the "habit of some" who choose to neglect their involvement in the body of Christ, we are reminded that beyond the goal of worship and teaching, the church is also a place where we are supposed to "stir up one another to love and good works" and be active in "encouraging one another, and all the more as you see the Day drawing near" (Hebrews 10:24-25). You might feel like giving yourself a pass on church when you are suffering, but in fact that is when you need the stirring up and the encouragement more than ever. Instead of cutting back your participation, you would be wise to step it up. God has a way of uniquely ministering to you when you obediently get plugged in to the meetings and programs of your church. Don't let your pain keep you from it—instead, let your pain help drive you there.

Connect with Christians

You may decide to dutifully attend church when you are suffering, only to short-circuit the benefits of participating by putting on a brave face, burying any signs of your pain, and simply putting in your time without ever truly connecting with others. While I am not suggesting you lead into every conversation in the lobby of the church with the full story behind the pain in your life, I *am* saying that if you come and go from your meetings with other Christians and never give them an opportunity to share in your struggles, then something is wrong. This is why church has to involve more than those times when your chairs are side-by-side. You have to participate in the programs within your church where your chairs are turned face-to-face. Whether it is a small group, a discipleship program, or a fellowship meal, you need to attend meetings or events where you get to share with one another and pray together.

The apostle Paul was no crybaby or hypochondriac, but when he was struggling he wanted his brothers in Christ to share his burden. Note the vulnerable transparency in this opening chapter of 2 Corinthians:

> We do not want you to be unaware, brothers, of the affliction we experienced in Asia. For we were so utterly burdened beyond our strength that we despaired of life itself. Indeed, we felt that we had received the sentence of death. But that was to make us rely not on ourselves but on God who raises the dead. He delivered us from such a deadly peril, and he will deliver us. On him we have set *our hope that he will deliver us again. You also must help us by prayer, so that many will give thanks on our behalf for the blessing granted us through the prayers of many* (1:8-11).

Paul did *not* want those in the church to be unaware of his burden. That is the exact opposite of what many Christians do—they work to ensure that others *are* unaware of their burdens. Paul was not known for exaggerating, which shows the great vulnerability of his prayer request. He said that he "despaired of life itself" and that he and his ministry partners "felt that [they] had received the sentence of death." That's a big admission, which obviously wasn't for dramatic effect. Paul was sharing with his fellow Christians that this current trial made him feel like dying.

I wonder how open and honest you have been with your brothers and sisters in Christ about the pain you are going through—not just the circumstances of your trial, but also the despair of your heart. We need each other in our suffering. We not only need to stay involved in church, but once we are there we have to be willing to share our heartfelt prayer requests and relay the depth of our pain. If that hasn't been the culture of your church, your small group, or your relationships at church, your purposed conversations can begin to change that. How pleased God will be when your church becomes more of a place where hurting people are strengthened, comforted, and encouraged.

> We need each other in our suffering.

Enlist Prayer Partners

Paul's transparency regarding his burden in 2 Corinthians was in part to gather prayer partners to help carry him through his trial. I love the vivid way he puts this request: "You also must help us by prayer" (1:11). We gain great emotional and spiritual strength when we know that people are lifting up our burdens before God in their prayers. Paul saw a great advantage in this multiplication of prayer on his behalf.

Have you boldly and forthrightly said to those in your church, "You must help me by prayer"? Imagine your own response if someone came to you, confessed his pain and said, "Please help me with your prayers." I don't know a genuine Christian who wouldn't find that opportunity a great privilege! Don't be shy about this. Follow the pattern of the apostle Paul and bravely ask individuals to join a growing team of prayer partners to help carry you through your trial.

Paul sent Titus, his ministry companion, hundreds of miles across the dangerous first-century landscape to *inform* the Corinthians of his burden and to ask them to pray. With all the technological advantages we possess, what do you think the early Christians would think about us withdrawing, circling the wagons, and failing to even send an email or a text message to ask our fellow believers to pray for us? Asking for prayer has never been easier. In your church there may already be many who have given themselves to the task of praying for those who are hurting. They just need to hear from you. Some churches call this a *prayer team* or a *prayer chain*—individuals who will immediately take your concerns and begin lifting them up before our powerful and merciful God. Make the call.

Strangely enough, an unfortunate excuse for not making the call may be found in something Paul said. Notice his very hopeful tone in 2 Corinthians 1. He confidently expected God to work out the whole situation he was facing. He said, "[God] delivered us from such a deadly peril, and he will deliver us. On him we have set our hope that he will deliver us again" (verse 10). That kind of honest optimism may reside in your heart. You may think, *Why should I get everybody all wrapped up in my problem, and reveal my strained feelings of pain and hurt, when I am quite sure that in time God is going to work it all out and get me through it?* If that is your reason for not sharing your burden with other Christians, it is a poor one.

Optimism and strong faith in God did not stop Paul from sharing his heart. One of the reasons he made his trials known was "so that many will give thanks on our behalf for the blessing granted us through the prayers of many" (verse 11). It was not only that he knew those prayers were instrumental in ushering in his relief, but also because he optimistically anticipated that when God did bring relief many more could rejoice in God's answers to their prayers.

I can remember the temptation twelve years ago of keeping the bad news of that ultrasound to ourselves—and sharing it only with our family and closest friends. But we quickly recalled this passage in 2 Corinthians and knew that whatever God was going to do in this crisis, we needed as many prayer partners in our lives as we could round up. And when the doctor's initial prognosis of death turned into a live birth, and the subsequent prognosis of an infant death and acute retardation turned into a tenacious eleven-year-old girl who is doing better than I did in school, many people now rejoice and give thanks to God.

Share your burden and assemble a team of prayer partners! There is no adequate excuse for not doing this.

Locate Experienced Sufferers

Another benefit of getting to church, connecting with Christians, sharing your burdens, and building a prayer team is that you will soon discover that not only are there others who suffer with equally severe pains, but some have problems very similar to your own. Your trials are rarely, if ever, unique. Depending on the size of your church, there is likely someone who has gone through, is going through, or knows someone who has gone through the very thing that you are facing.

As we discussed in chapter 8, suffering prepares you for future ministry, and it is important at this point to recognize that the suffering of some of the Christians in your church has already prepared them to minister to you. Just prior to Paul's prayer request in 2 Corinthians 1, he said that God "comforts us in all our affliction, so that we may be able to comfort those who are in any affliction, with the comfort with which we ourselves are comforted by God" (2 Corinthians 1:3-7). Those who have endured similar challenges and losses have learned to provide God's comfort to you. Find them. Discover what they have learned. Ask them how they gained perspective, comfort, and strength as they travelled the road you are now on.

You don't have to locate spiritual giants or profoundly wise people. Just find Christians who know what it is to suffer, and you will see how God can use them in your life to help

> The Lord uses ordinary people, even those more spiritually inexperienced than you, as his conduits of comfort and support.

you walk through your pain. Don't consider yourself some kind of super spiritual Christian who can't find anyone more mature than yourself who is able to minister to you. I find too many people like that in the church—individuals who delude themselves into thinking that because of their maturity they are left to sit by themselves on a park bench and God will have to spiritually provide all his comfort to them directly. As I'll soon get to, there is a place for solitary time with God, but what I am saying here is that the Lord uses ordinary people, even those more spiritually inexperienced than you, as his conduits of comfort and support.

You'd have to agree that it must have been hard for Paul to find someone to look up to spiritually in the first-century church, and yet he tells the Corinthians that when he and his companions were afflicted and fearful, "God, who comforts the downcast, comforted us by the coming of Titus" (2 Corinthians 7:6). Here the young understudy of the apostle Paul became God's conduit of great comfort and encouragement to him when he was hurting. God uses ordinary Christians to get his encouragement, strength, and peace into your life. Find some people in your church who know what it is to suffer, and allow them to be God's comfort in your life.

Engage in God's Word

When I was a new Christian, I remember hearing an old line being bandied about that has repeatedly surfaced in my memory at strategic times during my trials. It simply states, "A Bible that is falling apart is probably owned by someone who isn't." When I heard that pithy phrase I envisioned the tattered, crusty, dog-eared Bibles that the old-timers in our church carried around. At the time when I first heard that line my Bible was crisp, clean, and pristine. I remember thinking how important it would be for that Book to become well-worn by

> The spiritual exercise of Bible reading is important...even more so when our lives are turbulent.

my intake of it. Especially if I was ever going to be spiritually strong and prepared to navigate whatever struggles and disappointments would be a part of God's plan for my life.

That important correlation didn't originate from a modern Christian platitude. The apostle John said, "I write to you, young men, because you are strong, and the word of God abides in you, and you have overcome the evil one" (1 John 2:14). So much is at stake in how you handle the trials in your life. Satan would love to have you fret, worry, grow bitter, and chronically complain. Your resistance, faith, and strength, as John wrote, will be due in large part to how much of the Bible gets in your mind, heart, and life. That has to be your goal, and therefore its intake must be a prioritized part of your daily life.

1. Read It—All of It

When we are suffering we may not feel like picking up our Bibles, but doing so will make a bigger difference than we can imagine. The spiritual exercise of Bible reading is important, not only when our lives are on a steady course, but even more so when our lives are turbulent. We need the big picture of God's inspired library—the ups and downs, the battles and the wars, the prophecies and their fulfillments. Reading of them daily, all of them, from beginning to end is the way to get this perspective.

I am always surprised by how many Christians claim to base their eternal destiny on the message of God's Word but have never read the whole message. Surprisingly, it takes only about 50 hours to read the entire Bible. You could read it out loud to someone in less than 80 hours. There are 1189 chapters in it. Even if you only read three-and-a-half chapters a day, you'd get through the whole Bible in less than a year. In the time it takes to shower and brush your teeth each day, you could be storing up the entire Bible in your heart.

As you read about the Old Testament ceremonial regulations, the exodus from Egypt, and the kings of Judah, you might wonder what it all has to do with your personal pain and suffering. Well, here is God's promise regarding his Book—even those dusty parts of the Old Testament:

> Whatever was written in former days was written for our instruction, that through endurance and through the encouragement of the Scriptures we might have hope. May the God of endurance and encouragement grant you to live in such harmony with one another, in accord with Christ Jesus, that together you may with one voice glorify the God and Father of our Lord Jesus Christ (Romans 15:4-6).

It is not hard to see how desperately we need encouragement, hope, and endurance when we are suffering. If so, then we should know that it's the things "written in former days" in God's inspired library that have the power to bring them into our lives. So let's get in the Word. Let's start reading it today and keep on reading it every day. In our modern world it may not be a tattered physical Bible. Instead, the Bible will be the top title on our electronic reading devices, the most highlighted digital book, or the most frequented app on our phones—in whatever format, a constant immersion in God's Word will characterize a life that is unlikely to fall apart when life gets tough.

2. Study It

Reading through the Bible gives us a 40,000-foot view of God's work in and through history, but it is important to realize that every small portion of God's Word is packed with insight and profound wisdom. It is one thing to put our feet up and read through chapter after chapter of the Bible each day, but it is an increasing challenge, particularly when we are suffering, to roll up our sleeves and expend the energy digging into one or two verses of Scripture. But let me assure you, it is always worth the effort.

Consider that the Bible is often equated with food for the Christian life. The simple truths found in the Bible are said to be the Christian's *milk* (1 Peter 2:2), while the more difficult and complex truths mined from the Scriptures are called the *meat* (Hebrews 5:11-14). Imagine now that someone came up to you and said they were physically struggling and hurting in life, and by the way, they hadn't had anything to eat since they started feeling bad. I suppose, as with physical ailments, there are times we might not feel up to having a big spiritual meal, but if in our seasons of suffering we do not dig into God's Word, ingesting not only an ample supply of God's spiritual milk but also a healthy portion of the meat of the Word, then there won't be much hope for a spiritual recovery.

If our faith in God is to remain strong, and our spiritual lives are to remain vibrant as we make our way through our current trial, then we have to get serious about seeking our sustenance from the Bible. When we get under the surface of a text and dig deeper into the nourishing principles of Scripture it will revive us, empower us, and sustain us. Paul said as we work to receive the Word of God, it gets to work in us:

> We also thank God constantly for this, that when you received the word of God, which you heard from us, you accepted it not as the word of men but as what it really is, the word of God, which is at work in you believers (1 Thessalonians 2:13).

So pick a consistent time and place, and determine to keep your appointment to study the Bible, allowing your new discoveries to fuel your spirit. I am sure that, like the psalmist, you will recognize the inestimable value of that time, and will look back on it, saying to the Lord: "If your law had not been my delight, I would have perished in my affliction" (Psalm 119:92).

3. Memorize It

Far too many Christians think that memorizing verses from the Bible is a Sunday school activity for our children. Nothing could be further from the truth. Not only is this essential for our kids, it is also critically important for us adults—especially when we suffer. Unless we commit sections of God's Word to memory, we will certainly fail to recall them in those crucial moments of painful testing.

When Jesus was under attack by Satan in the desert, his victory was repeatedly won through the recital of Scripture verses. As we observe Jesus in this critical and vulnerable episode of his life, we see the indispensable example of having various parts of the Bible committed to memory. Peter wrote, "Since therefore Christ suffered in the flesh, arm yourselves with the same way of thinking" (1 Peter 4:1). Clearly in this assault on Jesus' faith, his "way of thinking" included a pattern of recalling and employing appropriate truths from the Bible.

Seeing Christ shrewdly fight the devil's attempts to lure him into doubt and compromise should motivate us to do to the same. John tells us that "whoever says he abides in [Christ] ought to walk in the same way in which he walked" (1 John 2:6). In the case of Jesus' suffering in the desert, it would be impossible to "walk as he walked" without a practice of memorizing verses from the Bible.

> Committing verses to memory...will prove to be the difference between victory and despair, confidence and hopelessness.

David could not have said it more clearly: "I have stored up your word in my heart, that I might not sin against you" (Psalm 119:11). If you have not been memorizing Scripture, now is the time to start. Write down a verse or two from your reading or study that has recently ministered to you. Write them on a card, a sticky note, or a white board and start working to ingrain the wording and meaning of those verses into your memory. When you've got one verse down pat, pick another, then three or four more. You will find that committing verses to memory will enable you to utilize these important truths at pivotal crossroads. And they will prove to be the difference between victory and despair, confidence and hopelessness.

Alone Time with God

The Old Testament prophets accurately foretold that Jesus would be "a man of sorrows, and acquainted with grief" (Isaiah 53:3). When Christ arrived hundreds of years later, the Gospel writers noted not only his many distresses and hardships, but also his pattern of finding the needed sustenance in private fellowship with his Father day by day. Certainly the four Gospels show us that Jesus was not a recluse or hermit. Notice how often, amid Christ's extraordinarily busy schedule, we see this important habit:

> After he had dismissed the crowds, he went up on the mountain by himself to pray. When evening came, he was there alone (Matthew 14:23).

> Rising very early in the morning, while it was still dark, he departed and went out to a desolate place, and there he prayed. And Simon and those who were with him searched for him (Mark 1:35-36).

> After he had taken leave of them, he went up on the mountain to pray (Mark 6:46).

> When it was day, he departed and went into a desolate place. And the people sought him... (Luke 4:42).

> He would withdraw to desolate places and pray (Luke 5:16).

> In these days he went out to the mountain to pray, and all night he continued in prayer to God (Luke 6:12).

> Jesus withdrew again to the mountain by himself (John 6:15).

If Jesus Christ relied on this regular practice of alone time with the Father, how much more should our lives be characterized by the same! If, as we saw earlier, we are to "walk in the same way in which he walked" (1 John 2:6), then creating and guarding these uninterrupted quiet times with God is a must. It may infringe on our sleep, it may take time from our families, it may impede on other activities that we value, but it cannot be forsaken if we are to have any hope of finding spiritual strength amid our personal battles.

Besides our intake of Scripture, we may wonder what these solitary times will entail. Here are a few basic ingredients.

1. Scriptural Meditation

It is unfortunate that today's Eastern religions have hijacked and effectively redefined the word *meditation* for most modern Christians. Far from emptying our minds, chanting mantras, or engaging in specialized breathing techniques, biblical meditation engages the mind to actively ponder the meaning and application of Scripture. It is the kind of practice that focuses our mind and heart on the truth of a particular passage so that we soberly consider its various implications. The Old Testament Hebrew word that translates to "meditate" is *Hāgâh,* and means to mutter or recite. It is sometimes used to describe the lowing of animals or the cooing of doves. It is what we might hear as someone reads to himself, intently poring over a particular line of text.

In the Bible the practice of scriptural meditation is shown to be one of the keys to finding spiritual vibrancy within difficult situations. Listen to David's description of the one who regularly meditates on Scripture:

> Blessed is the man who walks not in the counsel of the wicked, nor stands in the way of sinners, nor sits in the seat of scoffers; but his delight is in the law of the LORD, and on his law he meditates day and night. He is like a

tree planted by streams of water that yields its fruit in its
season, and its leaf does not wither. In all that he does,
he prospers. The wicked are not so, but are like chaff that
the wind drives away (Psalm 1:1-4).

The contrast depicted for us in Psalm 1 is stark. The godless are
viewed as the to-be-discarded husks of wheat—the dried up "chaff."
The blessed man is viewed as a fruitful tree that finds its sustenance
under the surface, transplanted to drink in its nourishment from the
streams of water. This picture reminds me of the Coachella Valley,
which is just a couple hours from the Southern California beaches.
This area receives less than three inches of rain per year. It has a dry
and extremely arid climate. It is a harsh environment, with tempera-
tures routinely above 100 degrees. Yet as you drive east out Interstate
10 approaching this valley, you suddenly notice the desert blossom
with rows of palm trees, hundreds of swimming pools, and lush golf
courses. The scorching heat and the months without rain do not
inhibit this thriving desert. The Coachella Valley is quietly hydrated
by a giant underground aquifer—loaded with sustaining "streams
of water."

Of course that is the principle this passage is trying to highlight—
namely, that a divinely blessed, vibrant, and thriving spirit is not one
that is dependent on *good weather*. Instead, this Christian is one who
can be fruitful and spiritually healthy based on the unseen nourishment that comes from God and the practice of meditating on his
Word. That's the kind of true prosperity that we long for. And it is
the promise held out to us as we make and guard our uninterrupted
time with the Lord, pondering, contemplating, and reflecting on
his life-giving Word.

2. Heartfelt Prayer

Often when we read the Gospel writers' descriptions of Christ's
alone time with his Father, prayer was the centerpiece. This seems

obvious, but we should briefly build on what we discussed in chapter 7 and consider for a moment the importance of private, undistracted, heartfelt prayer.

In our quiet times with God, it is essential that we hear from him through our reading, study, and meditation of his Word. But the amazing reality is that God also wants to hear from us. What an undervalued privilege it is to have the attention of the God of the universe when we pray. Moses reminded the children of Israel that the availability of deity is no small thing. He told them that not only did Israel have the benefit of God's revealed words, but he asked the people, "What great nation is there that has a god so near to it as the LORD our God is to us, whenever we call upon him?" (Deuteronomy 4:7-8).

All throughout the Bible we learn that God is not looking for some emotionless recital of a set of prefabricated prayers. Particularly when life hurts, the Bible calls us to "trust in him at all times, O people; pour out your heart before him; God is a refuge for us" (Psalm 62:8). That kind of praying will sound far different from anything we would hear at a Sunday worship service. This sort of solitary praying is the raw and plaintive expression of our hearts. Even Jesus was known for this kind of praying during his sufferings. The writer of Hebrews said,

> In the days of his flesh, Jesus offered up prayers and supplications, with loud cries and tears, to him who was able to save him from death, and he was heard because of his reverence (Hebrews 5:7).

Have your prayers been too restrained and wooden? I am not talking about losing our sense of reverence and respect for the almighty God, but I am calling for a kind of praying that doesn't hold back our hurts and deep concerns. When Paul wrote to the Philippians on the topic of anxiety, he told them to replace worry with earnest appeals to God (4:6). He ended his instructions by saying simply: "Let your requests be made known to God" (verse 6). Of course, making them "known to God" is not for his enlightenment. God's concern is for us to get our requests out of our hearts and mouths.

So let's make our requests plain and forthright. There is something internally helpful about being vocal and very clear with God about our problems, as well as our ideas of the potential solutions. We cannot walk away from a prayer time like that with any doubt that God knows all about the problems and every perfect solution. Sure, God knew all of it before we ever informed him of those thoughts and opened our mouths. But God has a way of rearranging our hearts when our specific prayers remind us that he intimately knows everything about our struggles.

It is no coincidence that the next verse in Philippians 4 gives us a look at one of the primary things that we have been in pursuit of all through our times of pain. After talking about this important outpouring of our hearts to God, Paul wrote, "And the peace of God, which surpasses all understanding, will guard your hearts and your minds in Christ Jesus" (verse 7). The specific answers and the resolve of our problem may be long in coming—but the immediate result of this kind of clear-minded and heartfelt praying is a flood of peace. It is an inner calm that "surpasses all understanding" to our onlookers, because what is seen on the outside may still be that the disease is having a heyday, the bank account is still empty, or the trial still looks as bad as it did before, *but* in our alone time with God our hearts have shifted the burden and we are reassured that our caring Father knows our need.

3. Godly Resolves

The final thing that I would suggest for you to include in your private time with God is a regular thoughtful expression of godly resolves. Recently in Christianity, the climate has shifted on this topic, and what used to be a natural conclusion to a Christian's quiet time is now frequently being neglected, if not altogether avoided. I realize we live in a culture that increasingly seeks to avoid commitment whenever possible. Few people want longer contracts on their cell phones, more pledges at their workplace, or more pages of covenants on their home loan docs. But when we read the Bible or study church history, it is hard to avoid the vital role that vows, promises, commitments, and resolves have played in the lives of God's people.

Though his résumé was filled with years of oppression and mistreatment, David was remembered by the Old Testament worshippers as one who frequently made godly resolutions during his trials. They sang of him:

> Remember, O LORD, in David's favor,
> all the hardships he endured,
> how he swore to the LORD
> and vowed to the Mighty One of Jacob (Psalm 132:1-2).

Especially when we are suffering, it is extremely helpful to come out of our time of communion with the Father having laid out a godly resolution or determination that will help direct our thoughts, attitudes, and decisions. The fog of pain can drive us to make snap decisions that we often later regret. The frequent crafting and expression of godly resolves to the Lord can keep our emotions from taking over when the pressure is on, our hearts are weighed down, or the unprincipled people in our lives are advising a compromised fix for our pain.

It might be as simple as writing out and expressing to God a resolve to keep your focus on the coming kingdom of Christ as you prepare for an afternoon doctor's appointment. Or it might be an all-day pledge to pray at the top of every hour for insight on how your current season of suffering can be utilized as a means to minister to those in your church. It could even be a firm promise to God that you will not withdraw from church attendance, and that you will sign up and participate in a small group. Get in the habit of noting the things that God is showing you in his Word, especially those important truths related to your current crisis, and make your prayerful resolves, asking God for the enablement to carry them through.

Day by Day

In the initial months following the revised prenatal diagnosis of Stephanie's spina bifida and hydrocephalus life was particularly difficult and filled with uncertainty for Carlynn and me. The hurt increased, and the busyness of life never let up. In the middle of a particularly busy week my exhausted wife opened her calendar and blurted out, "So what's our plan for yesterday?" I gave her a bewildered look and said, "Now there's a profound question that I've never been asked before; I have no plans for yesterday." We both got a good laugh out of the misspoken question.

Later that night, though, her words brought my mind back to the counsel of Christ. He told us that we can't change yesterday, we're not to worry about tomorrow, and that when it comes to life, "sufficient for the day is its own trouble" (Matthew 6:34).

> Will we seek to look beyond the pain to the prize that awaits those who trust God?

The question for us is this: What will we do with *today*? Today will we allow our painful circumstances to define our lives and direct our hearts? Will we get mad at God and accuse him of wrongdoing? Will we fret, complain, and be bitter? Or will we turn to the One who can change our hearts? Will we invest in the people who can bring us comfort? Will we place our confidence in and draw our perspective from God's reliable Word? And will we seek to look beyond the pain to the prize that awaits those who trust God and resolve to bring glory to his name in good times and bad?

I commend you to the grace of God. I pray your trials result in glory to God, good for his church, and a transformed character and a mature faith for you. And may your daily spiritual disciplines yield fruit in every aspect of your life as you seek his face and his will from day to day. The light of God's relief will dawn. "Weeping may tarry for the night, but joy comes with the morning" (Psalm 30:5). Trust him; he will care for you.

> After you have suffered a little while, the God of all grace, who has called you to his eternal glory in Christ, will himself restore, confirm, strengthen, and establish you. To him be the dominion forever and ever. Amen (1 Peter 5:10-11).

Biblical Lifelines

Nothing can bring comfort and perspective like God's own words. So allow me to step out of the way and let you take in God's voice from the pages of his Book. I encourage you to prayerfully read and meditate on these excerpts from the Bible. No matter what you are facing, it is my hope that a thoughtful reading of the following pages will profoundly minister to your heart, and strengthen your trust in Christ as you navigate the tough times.

The Power of God's Word

The word of God is living and active, sharper than any two-edged sword, piercing to the division of soul and of spirit, of joints and of marrow, and discerning the thoughts and intentions of the heart. And no creature is hidden from his sight, but all are naked and exposed to the eyes of him to whom we must give account (Hebrews 4:12-13).

The precepts of the LORD are right, rejoicing the heart; the commandment of the LORD is pure, enlightening the eyes; the fear of the LORD is clean, enduring forever; the rules of the LORD are true, and righteous altogether. More to be desired are they than gold, even much fine gold; sweeter also than honey and drippings of the honeycomb. Moreover, by them is your servant warned; in keeping them there is great reward (Psalm 19:8-11).

Blessed is the man who walks not in the counsel of the wicked, nor stands in the way of sinners, nor sits in the seat of scoffers; but his delight is in the law of the LORD, and on his law he meditates day and night. He is like a tree planted by streams of water that yields its fruit in its season, and its leaf does not wither. In all that he does, he prospers (Psalm 1:1-3).

Put Your Hope in the Lord

Blessed is he whose help is the God of Jacob, whose hope is in the LORD his God, who made heaven and earth, the sea, and all that is in them, who keeps faith forever; who executes justice for the oppressed, who gives food to the hungry. The LORD sets the prisoners free; the LORD opens the eyes of the blind. The LORD lifts up those who are bowed down; the LORD loves the righteous. The LORD watches over the sojourners; he upholds the widow and the fatherless, but the way of the wicked he brings to ruin (Psalm 146:5-9).

In you, O LORD, do I take refuge; let me never be put to shame! In your righteousness deliver me and rescue me; incline your ear to me, and save me! Be to me a rock of refuge, to which I may continually come; you have given the command to save me, for you are my rock and my fortress. Rescue me, O my God, from the hand of the wicked, from the grasp of the unjust and cruel man. For you, O Lord, are my hope, my trust, O LORD, from my youth (Psalm 71:1-5).

May the LORD answer you in the day of trouble! May the name of the God of Jacob protect you! May he send you help from the sanctuary and give you support from Zion!…May he grant you your heart's desire and fulfill all your plans! May we shout for joy over your salvation, and in the name of our God set up our banners! May the LORD fulfill all your petitions! Now I know that the LORD saves his anointed; he will answer him from his holy heaven with the saving might of his right hand. Some trust in chariots and some in horses, but we trust in the name of the Lord our God. They collapse and fall, but we rise and stand upright (Psalm 20:1-8).

Our Powerful God

Yours, O Lord, is the greatness and the power and the glory and the victory and the majesty, for all that is in the heavens and in the earth is yours. Yours is the kingdom, O Lord, and you are exalted as head above all. Both riches and honor come from you, and you rule over all. In your hand are power and might, and in your hand it is to make great and to give strength to all (1 Chronicles 29:11-12).

Behold, there arose a great storm on the sea, so that the boat was being swamped by the waves; but he was asleep. And they went and woke him, saying, "Save us, Lord; we are perishing." And he said to them, "Why are you afraid, O you of little faith?" Then he rose and rebuked the winds and the sea, and there was a great calm. And the men marveled, saying, "What sort of man is this, that even winds and sea obey him?" (Matthew 8:24-27).

I do not cease to give thanks for you, remembering you in my prayers, that the God of our Lord Jesus Christ, the Father of glory, may give you the Spirit of wisdom and of revelation in the knowledge of him, having the eyes of your hearts enlightened, that you may know what is the hope to which he has called you, what are the riches of his glorious inheritance in the saints, and what is the immeasurable greatness of his power toward us who believe, according to the working of his great might that he worked in Christ when he raised him from the dead and seated him at his right hand in the heavenly places, far above all rule and authority and power and dominion, and above every name that is named, not only in this age but also in the one to come. And he put all things under his feet and gave him as head over all things to the church, which is his body, the fullness of him who fills all in all (Ephesians 1:16-23).

The Loving Concern of God

The steadfast love of the LORD never ceases; his mercies never come to an end; they are new every morning; great is your faithfulness. "The LORD is my portion," says my soul, "therefore I will hope in him." The LORD is good to those who wait for him, to the soul who seeks him. It is good that one should wait quietly for the salvation of the LORD (Lamentations 3:22-26).

I tell you, do not be anxious about your life, what you will eat or what you will drink, nor about your body, what you will put on. Is not life more than food, and the body more than clothing? Look at the birds of the air: they neither sow nor reap nor gather into barns, and yet your heavenly Father feeds them. Are you not of more value than they? And which of you by being anxious can add a single hour to his span of life? And why are you anxious about clothing? Consider the lilies of the field, how they grow: they neither toil nor spin, yet I tell you, even Solomon in all his glory was not arrayed like one of these. But if God so clothes the grass of the field, which today is alive and tomorrow is thrown into the oven, will he not much more clothe you, O you of little faith? Therefore do not be anxious, saying, "What shall we eat?" or "What shall we drink?" or "What shall we wear?" For the Gentiles seek after all these things, and your heavenly Father knows that you need them all. But seek first the kingdom of God and his righteousness, and all these things will be added to you. Therefore do not be anxious about tomorrow, for tomorrow will be anxious for itself. Sufficient for the day is its own trouble (Matthew 6:25-34).

I tell you, my friends, do not fear those who kill the body, and after that have nothing more that they can do. But I will warn you whom to fear: fear him who, after he has killed, has authority to cast into hell. Yes, I tell you, fear him! Are not five sparrows sold for two pennies? And not one of them is forgotten before God. Why, even the hairs of your head are all numbered. Fear not; you are of more value than many sparrows (Luke 12:4-7).

The Sympathy of Christ

Since then we have a great high priest who has passed through the heavens, Jesus, the Son of God, let us hold fast our confession. For we do not have a high priest who is unable to sympathize with our weaknesses, but one who in every respect has been tempted as we are, yet without sin. Let us then with confidence draw near to the throne of grace, that we may receive mercy and find grace to help in time of need (Hebrews 4:14-16).

They went to a place called Gethsemane. And he said to his disciples, "Sit here while I pray." And he took with him Peter and James and John, and began to be greatly distressed and troubled. And he said to them, "My soul is very sorrowful, even to death. Remain here and watch." And going a little farther, he fell on the ground and prayed that, if it were possible, the hour might pass from him. And he said, "Abba, Father, all things are possible for you. Remove this cup from me. Yet not what I will, but what you will" (Mark 14:32-36).

To this you have been called, because Christ also suffered for you, leaving you an example, so that you might follow in his steps. He committed no sin, neither was deceit found in his mouth. When he was reviled, he did not revile in return; when he suffered, he did not threaten, but continued entrusting himself to him who judges justly (1 Peter 2:21-23).

The Promise of Trials

To the woman he said, "I will surely multiply your pain in childbearing; in pain you shall bring forth children. Your desire shall be for your husband, and he shall rule over you." And to Adam he said, "Because you have listened to the voice of your wife and have eaten of the tree of which I commanded you, 'You shall not eat of it,' cursed is the ground because of you; in pain you shall eat of it all the days of your life; thorns and thistles it shall bring forth for you; and you shall eat the plants of the field. By the sweat of your face you shall eat bread, till you return to the ground, for out of it you were taken; for you are dust, and to dust you shall return" (Genesis 3:16-19).

"If the world hates you, know that it has hated me before it hated you. If you were of the world, the world would love you as its own; but because you are not of the world, but I chose you out of the world, therefore the world hates you. Remember the word that I said to you: 'A servant is not greater than his master.' If they persecuted me, they will also persecute you. If they kept my word, they will also keep yours. But all these things they will do to you on account of my name, because they do not know him who sent me" (John 15:18-21).

Let your manner of life be worthy of the gospel of Christ, so that whether I come and see you or am absent, I may hear of you that you are standing firm in one spirit, with one mind striving side by side for the faith of the gospel, and not frightened in anything by your opponents. This is a clear sign to them of their destruction, but of your salvation, and that from God. For it has been granted to you that for the sake of Christ you should not only believe in him but also suffer for his sake, engaged in the same conflict that you saw I had and now hear that I still have (Philippians 1:27-30).

Be patient, therefore, brothers, until the coming of the Lord. See how the farmer waits for the precious fruit of the earth, being patient about it, until it receives the early and the late rains. You also, be patient. Establish your hearts, for the coming of the Lord is at hand. Do not grumble against one another, brothers, so that you may not be judged; behold, the Judge is standing at the door. As an example of suffering and patience, brothers, take the prophets who spoke in the name of the Lord. Behold, we consider those blessed who remained steadfast. You have heard of the steadfastness of Job, and you have seen the purpose of the Lord, how the Lord is compassionate and merciful (James 5:7-11).

Blessed be the God and Father of our Lord Jesus Christ! According to his great mercy, he has caused us to be born again to a living hope through the resurrection of Jesus Christ from the dead, to an inheritance that is imperishable, undefiled, and unfading, kept in heaven for you, who by God's power are being guarded through faith for a salvation ready to be revealed in the last time. In this you rejoice, though now for a little while, if necessary, you have been grieved by various trials, so that the tested genuineness of your faith—more precious than gold that perishes though it is tested by fire—may be found to result in praise and glory and honor at the revelation of Jesus Christ. Though you have not seen him, you love him. Though you do not now see him, you believe in him and rejoice with joy that is inexpressible and filled with glory, obtaining the outcome of your faith, the salvation of your souls (1 Peter 1:3-9).

Bless our God, O peoples; let the sound of his praise be heard, who has kept our soul among the living and has not let our feet slip. For you, O God, have tested us; you have tried us as silver is tried. You brought us into the net; you laid a crushing burden on our backs; you let men ride over our heads; we went through fire and through water; yet you have brought us out to a place of abundance. I will come into your house with burnt offerings; I will perform my vows to you, that which my lips uttered and my mouth promised when I was in trouble. I will offer to you burnt offerings of fattened animals, with the smoke of the sacrifice of rams; I will make an offering of bulls and goats. Come and hear, all you who fear God, and I will tell what he has done for my soul. I cried to him with my mouth, and high praise was on my tongue. If I had cherished iniquity in my heart, the Lord would not have listened. But truly God has listened; he has attended to the voice of my prayer. Blessed be God, because he has not rejected my prayer or removed his steadfast love from me! (Psalm 66:8-20).

Our Call to Endure

Therefore, since we are surrounded by so great a cloud of witnesses, let us also lay aside every weight, and sin which clings so closely, and let us run with endurance the race that is set before us, looking to Jesus, the founder and perfecter of our faith, who for the joy that was set before him endured the cross, despising the shame, and is seated at the right hand of the throne of God. Consider him who endured from sinners such hostility against himself, so that you may not grow weary or fainthearted (Hebrews 12:1-3).

Count it all joy, my brothers, when you meet trials of various kinds, for you know that the testing of your faith produces steadfastness. And let steadfastness have its full effect, that you may be perfect and complete, lacking in nothing. If any of you lacks wisdom, let him ask God, who gives generously to all without reproach, and it will be given him (James 1:2-5).

Have you forgotten the exhortation that addresses you as sons? "My son, do not regard lightly the discipline of the Lord, nor be weary when reproved by him. For the Lord disciplines the one he loves, and chastises every son whom he receives." It is for discipline that you have to endure. God is treating you as sons. For what son is there whom his father does not discipline? If you are left without discipline, in which all have participated, then you are illegitimate children and not sons. Besides this, we have had earthly fathers who disciplined us and we respected them. Shall we not much more be subject to the Father of spirits and live? For they disciplined us for a short time as it seemed best to them, but he disciplines us for our good, that we may share his holiness. For the moment all discipline seems painful rather than pleasant, but later it yields the peaceful fruit of righteousness to those who have been trained by it (Hebrews 12:5-11).

The Support of God's Family

Blessed be the God and Father of our Lord Jesus Christ, the Father of mercies and God of all comfort, who comforts us in all our affliction, so that we may be able to comfort those who are in any affliction, with the comfort with which we ourselves are comforted by God. For as we share abundantly in Christ's sufferings, so through Christ we share abundantly in comfort too. If we are afflicted, it is for your comfort and salvation; and if we are comforted, it is for your comfort, which you experience when you patiently endure the same sufferings that we suffer. Our hope for you is unshaken, for we know that as you share in our sufferings, you will also share in our comfort. For we do not want you to be unaware, brothers, of the affliction we experienced in Asia. For we were so utterly burdened beyond our strength that we despaired of life itself. Indeed, we felt that we had received the sentence of death. But that was to make us rely not on ourselves but on God who raises the dead. He delivered us from such a deadly peril, and he will deliver us. On him we have set our hope that he will deliver us again. You also must help us by prayer, so that many will give thanks on our behalf for the blessing granted us through the prayers of many (2 Corinthians 1:3-11).

We were gentle among you, like a nursing mother taking care of her own children. So, being affectionately desirous of you, we were ready to share with you not only the gospel of God but also our own selves, because you had become very dear to us. For you remember, brothers, our labor and toil: we worked night and day, that we might not be a burden to any of you, while we proclaimed to you the gospel of God. You are witnesses, and God also, how holy and righteous and blameless was our conduct toward you believers. For you know how, like a father with his children, we exhorted each one of you and encouraged you and charged you to walk in a manner worthy of God, who calls you into his own kingdom and glory (1 Thessalonians 2:7-12).

Strengthen the weak hands, and make firm the feeble knees. Say to those who have an anxious heart, "Be strong; fear not! Behold, your God will come with vengeance, with the recompense of God. He will come and save you" (Isaiah 35:3-4).

God's Gracious Deliverance

Moses and the people of Israel sang this song to the LORD, saying, "I will sing to the LORD, for he has triumphed gloriously; the horse and his rider he has thrown into the sea. The LORD is my strength and my song, and he has become my salvation; this is my God, and I will praise him, my father's God, and I will exalt him. The LORD is a man of war; the LORD is his name. Pharaoh's chariots and his host he cast into the sea, and his chosen officers were sunk in the Red Sea. The floods covered them; they went down into the depths like a stone. Your right hand, O LORD, glorious in power, your right hand, O LORD, shatters the enemy. In the greatness of your majesty you overthrow your adversaries; you send out your fury; it consumes them like stubble. At the blast of your nostrils the waters piled up; the floods stood up in a heap; the deeps congealed in the heart of the sea. The enemy said, 'I will pursue, I will overtake, I will divide the spoil, my desire shall have its fill of them. I will draw my sword; my hand shall destroy them.' You blew with your wind; the sea covered them; they sank like lead in the mighty waters. Who is like you, O LORD, among the gods? Who is like you, majestic in holiness, awesome in glorious deeds, doing wonders?" (Exodus 15:1-11).

David spoke to the LORD the words of this song on the day when the LORD delivered him from the hand of all his enemies, and from the hand of Saul. He said, "The LORD is my rock and my fortress and my deliverer, my God, my rock, in whom I take refuge, my shield, and the horn of my salvation, my stronghold and my refuge, my savior; you save me from violence. I call upon the Lord, who is worthy to be praised, and I am saved from my enemies. For the waves of death encompassed me, the torrents of destruction assailed me; the cords of Sheol entangled me; the snares of death confronted me. In my distress I called upon the Lord; to my God I called. From his temple he heard my voice, and my cry came to his ears. Then the earth reeled and rocked; the foundations of the heavens trembled and quaked, because he was angry. Smoke went up from his nostrils, and devouring fire from his mouth; glowing coals flamed forth from him. He bowed the heavens and came down; thick darkness was under his feet. He rode on a cherub and flew; he was seen on the wings of the wind. He made darkness around him his canopy, thick clouds, a gathering of water. Out of the brightness before him coals of fire flamed forth. The Lord thundered from heaven, and the Most High uttered his voice. And he sent out arrows and scattered them; lightning, and routed them. Then the channels of the sea were seen; the foundations of the world were laid bare, at the rebuke of the Lord, at the blast of the breath of his nostrils. He sent from on high, he took me; he drew me out of many waters. He rescued me from my strong enemy, from those who hated me, for they were too mighty for me. They confronted me in the day of my calamity, but the Lord was my support. He brought me out into a broad place; he rescued me, because he delighted in me. The Lord dealt with me according to my righteousness; according to the cleanness of my hands he rewarded me (2 Samuel 22:1-21).

Jonah prayed to the Lord his God from the belly of the fish, saying, "I called out to the Lord, out of my distress, and he answered me; out of the belly of Sheol I cried, and you heard my voice. For you cast me into the deep, into the heart of the seas, and the flood surrounded me; all your waves and your billows passed over me. Then I said, 'I am driven away from your sight; yet I shall again look upon your holy temple.' The waters closed in over me to take my life; the deep surrounded me; weeds were wrapped about my head at the roots of the mountains. I went down to the land whose bars closed upon me forever; yet you brought up my life from the pit, O LORD my God. When my life was fainting away, I remembered the LORD, and my prayer came to you, into your holy temple. Those who pay regard to vain idols forsake their hope of steadfast love. But I with the voice of thanksgiving will sacrifice to you; what I have vowed I will pay. Salvation belongs to the LORD!" (Jonah 2:1-9).

When Suffering Is Prolonged

The LORD is my shepherd; I shall not want. He makes me lie down in green pastures. He leads me beside still waters. He restores my soul. He leads me in paths of righteousness for his name's sake. Even though I walk through the valley of the shadow of death, I will fear no evil, for you are with me; your rod and your staff, they comfort me. You prepare a table before me in the presence of my enemies; you anoint my head with oil; my cup overflows. Surely goodness and mercy shall follow me all the days of my life, and I shall dwell in the house of the LORD forever (Psalm 23:1-6).

As servants of God we commend ourselves in every way: by great endurance, in afflictions, hardships, calamities, beatings, imprisonments, riots, labors, sleepless nights, hunger; by purity, knowledge, patience, kindness, the Holy Spirit, genuine love; by truthful speech, and the power of God; with the weapons of righteousness for the right hand and for the left; through honor and dishonor, through slander and praise. We are treated as impostors, and yet are true; as unknown, and yet well known; as dying, and behold, we live; as punished, and yet not killed; as sorrowful, yet always rejoicing; as poor, yet making many rich; as having nothing, yet possessing everything (2 Corinthians 6:4-10).

After you have suffered a little while, the God of all grace, who has called you to his eternal glory in Christ, will himself restore, confirm, strengthen, and establish you. To him be the dominion forever and ever. Amen (1 Peter 5:10-11).

Our Need for Perspective

I consider that the sufferings of this present time are not worth comparing with the glory that is to be revealed to us. For the creation waits with eager longing for the revealing of the sons of God. For the creation was subjected to futility, not willingly, but because of him who subjected it, in hope that the creation itself will be set free from its bondage to corruption and obtain the freedom of the glory of the children of God. For we know that the whole creation has been groaning together in the pains of childbirth until now. And not only the creation, but we ourselves, who have the firstfruits of the Spirit, groan inwardly as we wait eagerly for adoption as sons, the redemption of our bodies. For in this hope we were saved. Now hope that is seen is not hope. For who hopes for what he sees? But if we hope for what we do not see, we wait for it with patience (Romans 8:18-25).

We are afflicted in every way, but not crushed; perplexed, but not driven to despair; persecuted, but not forsaken; struck down, but not destroyed; always carrying in the body the death of Jesus, so that the life of Jesus may also be manifested in our bodies. For we who live are always being given over to death for Jesus' sake, so that the life of Jesus also may be manifested in our mortal flesh...So we do not lose heart. Though our outer self is wasting away, our inner self is being renewed day by day. For this light momentary affliction is preparing for us an eternal weight of glory beyond all comparison, as we look not to the things that are seen but to the things that are unseen. For the things that are seen are transient, but the things that are unseen are eternal (2 Corinthians 4:8-11, 16-18).

I saw a new heaven and a new earth, for the first heaven and the first earth had passed away, and the sea was no more. And I saw the holy city, new Jerusalem, coming down out of heaven from God, prepared as a bride adorned for her husband. And I heard a loud voice from the throne saying, "Behold, the dwelling place of God is with man. He will dwell with them, and they will be his people, and God himself will be with them as their God. He will wipe away every tear from their eyes, and death shall be no more, neither shall there be mourning, nor crying, nor pain anymore, for the former things have passed away" (Revelation 21:1-4).

Notes

Chapter 1—Things Will Go Wrong

1. Laura Bush, *Spoken from the Heart* (New York: Scribner, 2010), p. 65.
2. D.A. Carson, *How Long, O Lord? Reflections on Suffering and Evil* (Grand Rapids, MI: Baker Academic, 2006), p. 99.
3. See Isaiah 40:4-5.
4. See Revelation 21:4.
5. John 4:4.
6. 2 Corinthians 12:1-10.
7. Hebrews 13:5; see also Matthew 28:20.
8. A.W. Tozer, *Born After Midnight* (Harrisburg, PA: Christian Publications, 1963), p. 140.
9. Matthew 16:24.
10. Matthew 7:13-14.
11. Ibid.
12. C.S. Lewis, *The Problem of Pain* (New York: HarperCollins, 1996), p. 91.

Chapter 2—The Pain You Can Change

1. Psalm 139:24.

Chapter 3—Shifting Your Focus Amid the Hurt

1. As cited by Fawn M. Brodie, *Thomas Jefferson: An Intimate History* (New York: W.W. Norton & Co., 1998), p. 173.

Chapter 4—Rethinking Fairness

1. Harold S. Kushner, *When Bad Things Happen to Good People* (New York: Avon Books, HarperCollins, 1981).

Chapter 5—Why Being Heavenly Minded Does a World of Good

1. C.S. Lewis, *Mere Christianity* (New York: Scribner, 1986), p. 106.
2. C.S. Lewis, *The Joyful Christian* (New York: Scribner, 1996), p. 138.

Chapter 6—The Patience that Comes from Hope

1. George Matheson, "O Love That Will Not Let Me Go" in *Hymns for the Living Church* (Carol Stream, IL: Hope Publishing Co., 1974), #351.
2. As quoted by Joni Eareckson Tada, *Glorious Intruder* (Portland, OR: Multnomah Press, 1989), p. 38.
3. Verses 22-25.
4. See the translation in *God's Word* (Grand Rapids, MI: World Publishing, 1995) and *Good News Bible, Today's English Version* (New York: American Bible Society, 1976).
5. See the translation in *The Holy Bible, New Century Version* (Dallas, TX: Word Publishing, 1991).
6. See the King James Version of the Bible in Exodus 34:6; Number 14:18; Psalm 86:15; Romans 9:22; Galatians 5:22; 2 Peter 3:9; et al.

Chapter 7—Learning to Pray Through the Pain

1. See http://wheels.blogs.nytimes.com/2010/05/28/mom-says-giving-birth-while-driving-was-no-big-deal/?_r=0.
2. Joseph Scriven, 1855.

Chapter 9—Faith in the Goodness of God

1. D.A. Carson, *Divine Sovereignty and Human Responsibility: Biblical Perspectives in Tension* (Eugene, OR: Wipf & Stock Publishers, 2002), pp. 220-21.
2. Lewis Sperry Chafer, "The Doctrine of Sin," *Bibliotheca Sacra* (Dallas, TX: Dallas Theological Seminary, 1936), vol. 93, no. 371.

Chapter 10—Reasons for Confidence No Matter What

1. C.S. Lewis, *A Grief Observed* (New York: HarperOne, 2001), p. 1.
2. Martin Luther, "A Mighty Fortress Is Our God," circa 1529.

Chapter 11—God's Unchanging Love in a Turbulent World

1. Bruce K. Waltke, *Finding the Will of God: A Pagan Notion?* (Grand Rapids, MI: Eerdmans Publishing, 1995), p. 15.

Other Good Harvest House Reading

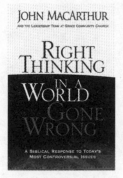

Right Thinking in a World Gone Wrong
John MacArthur, General Editor

One of the greatest challenges facing Christians today is the powerful influence of secular thinking. This makes it difficult to know where to stand on today's most talked-about issues, including political activism, environmentalism, homosexual marriage, abortion, disasters and epidemics, immigration, and more. A great resource for biblical answers to the tough questions.

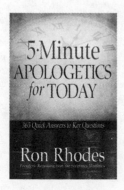

5-Minute Apologetics for Today
Ron Rhodes

Would you like to strengthen your understanding of the basics of the Christian faith? In just five minutes a day, you can read concise explanations that deal with difficult Bible verses, arguments people use against God and Christianity, the problem of evil, end-times prophecy, and more. A helpful topical index makes this a handy resource you'll turn to again and again.